50 Favourite Bible Stories

Hi! This is Cliff saying how much I'm looking forward to revisiting this selection of Bible stories from the Old and New Testaments. The Bible really is a remarkable book, you know. For no matter how many times you hear it or read its pages, it always seems to say something that's real and relevant for life today. The fact that it was written nearly 2000 years ago doesn't seem to matter! It just has a knack of being up to date – well, about everything! So whatever age you are as you listen out there, I do hope you'll enjoy this selection of readings. And most of all, I hope they'll make you think – and that at the end you might even want to explore some more about the book which really has shaped history and changed lives.

Recorded at Retiro Recording Studios, Moncarapacho, Algarve, Portugal.
Thanks to Trevor Holman.

For Malcolm Prince – because he has always wanted his own book.

Sincere thanks to Paul Clifford, Lois Rock, Kirsten Etheridge and Philippa Frewin
of Lion for making every stage of this book (from commissioning via editing to design)
such a pleasurable adventure; to Stephen Waterhouse for his visually inspired and joyous
collaboration; to Bill Latham at the CRO and (as always)
Vivien Green and David Weeks. *Brian Sibley*

For my inspirational Mum and Dad,
Alan and Cherie Waterhouse. *Stephen Waterhouse*

Cliff Richard © 2008 Vox Rock Ltd
Text copyright © 2008 Brian Sibley
Illustrations copyright © 2008 Stephen Waterhouse
This edition copyright © 2008 Lion Hudson
The moral rights of the author and illustrator
have been asserted
A Lion Children's Book
an imprint of
Lion Hudson plc
Wilkinson House, Jordan Hill Road,
Oxford OX2 8DR, England
www.lionhudson.com
ISBN 978 0 7459 6061 6
First edition 2008
1 3 5 7 9 10 8 6 4 2 0
All rights reserved
The Lord's Prayer from Common Worship: Services and Prayers
for the Church of England (Church House Publishing, 2000) is
copyright © The English Language Liturgical Consultation, 1988
and is reproduced by permission of the publishers.
A catalogue record for this book is available
from the British Library
Typeset in 18/23 Lapidary 333 BT
Printed and bound in Singapore

50 FAVOURITE
BIBLE STORIES

Retold by Brian Sibley

Illustrated by Stephen Waterhouse

LION
CHILDREN'S

CONTENTS

THE OLD TESTAMENT

THE NEW TESTAMENT

THE OLD TESTAMENT

1 IN THE BEGINNING

Everything, everywhere, began with God. There was once a time – long before time itself even started – when there was nothing in our world except swirling waters and total darkness.

But God was there. A moment came when he said, 'Let there be light!' and, suddenly, light streamed through the darkness – and God began creating the world that we now know.

God started by making the light and darkness into day and night, and putting the sky in place. Then he pushed back the waters and heaped up the land in order to make sea and earth so that trees and plants could begin growing on the earth and start producing flowers, fruits and seeds.

With each new day, God took pleasure in seeing his creation take shape. He made all the stars and the planets of the universe, the fiery sun to give warmth to the earth during the day, and the cool, pale moon to give light at night.

Next, God made the seas swim and swarm with fish and all kinds of sea creatures, while the skies all over the earth were filled with birdsong and the sound of beating wings.

Then all kinds of animals began to appear on the earth – from big, slow, lumbering ones to small, quick, furry ones. There were animals that ran, crawled, slithered, hopped, jumped, leaped and galloped. There were animals that roared, trumpeted, bellowed, mooed, snorted, bleated, barked, meowed and squeaked.

And then, when everything else was complete, God decided to make human beings – a man and a woman. God made them to be like himself, and he blessed them and put them in charge of his whole creation so that they could care for this perfect world that he had made.

His work finished, God sat back, took a long look at everything and decided that it was good. Very good.

2 THE GARDEN OF EDEN

God made a man and a woman to live in the world he had created. They were named Adam and Eve, and God gave them a beautiful garden in which to live.

God's garden was called Eden and it was filled with a great many trees. All of them had branches hung with the most delicious and luscious fruits.

In the very centre of the garden stood two great trees: one was the Tree of Life and the other was the Tree of the Knowledge of What is Good and What is Bad.

God told Adam,
'You can eat the
fruits of all of the
trees in the garden *except* those
that grow on the Tree of the
Knowledge of What is Good and What
is Bad, because if you eat the fruit of that
tree you will die.'

Adam and Eve lived in Eden, looking after the
trees and plants and caring for the animals, and their life was happy.
They wore no clothes, but they were not embarrassed and saw
nothing wrong in being naked.

Then one day, a sly, slithery snake sidled into the garden and
spoke to Eve. 'Are there any trees,' it asked, 'from which you are
not allowed to eat the fruit?'

'Only one,' Eve replied. 'God has said that we mustn't eat the
fruit of the Tree of the Knowledge of What is Good and What is
Bad. If we do, we will die.'

The snake sniggered. 'Of course you won't die!' it hissed. 'God
only told you that because he knows that if you eat the fruit you
will know everything that he knows!'

Once the snake had said this, Eve saw just how ripe and juicy the
fruit looked. The more she thought about it, the more she began to
think how good it would be to be as wise as God.

Eventually, the temptation was too strong and Eve picked one
of the fruits, ate some of it and then gave some to Adam.

No sooner had they both eaten the fruit than they saw that they were naked. At once they gathered fig leaves and tied them together to cover themselves.

They suddenly realized that they were wrong to have disobeyed God. When, that evening, God came walking through his garden, they ran away and hid among the trees. But God called to them, and finally they had to come out of hiding and tell God what had happened. Adam blamed Eve, and Eve said it was the snake's fault because it had tricked her, but it was too late for excuses…

'Because of what you have done,' God told them, 'you cannot live with me in my garden any longer. Now you will have to go out into the world. You will have children. You will have to work long and hard to provide food for yourselves and your family until eventually you grow old and, one day, die.'

So Adam and Eve left the beautiful garden for ever, but God made them clothes out of animal skins to keep them warm. Although they no longer lived with God, he never stopped loving them because – even though they had disobeyed him – God had created them and they were his children.

3 THE GREAT FLOOD

After leaving God's garden, Adam and Eve had children and then they in turn had children, and so it went on for hundreds of years, until people were living all over the world.

Just as Adam and Eve had done wrong in disobeying God, many of the people who came after them did all kinds of bad things to one another and stopped listening to God or even believing in God.

All this made God very unhappy and he began to wish that he had never made the world in the first place. In fact, God eventually decided to get rid of everything, all the people and all the animals and birds, and start again.

There was only one person who was living a good life – and that was a farmer called Noah, so one day God spoke to him. 'Noah,' he said, 'I want you and your sons, Shem, Ham and Japheth, to build me a boat.'

Now Noah had always believed in and trusted God, but he couldn't understand why he was supposed to build a boat when he lived nowhere near the sea. God explained that he was planning to send a great flood that would wash away everything on the face of the earth – except for whatever was safe and sound inside Noah's boat.

Then God gave Noah all the details about the size of the boat and it was clear that it was going to be huge. God explained that it had to be big because, in addition to Noah and his wife and Noah's sons and their wives, they were going to be carrying a very important cargo.

'I want you to take two of all the animals and birds that you can find,' said God, 'a male and female of each, so that they will all survive the flood. And do not forget to take enough food for everyone to eat.'

It took a long time to build the great boat and almost as long to round up all the animals and birds. But at last, everyone and everything was inside the boat and the doors were shut tight. It was then that the first few light drops of rain began to pitter-patter on the roof. Before long, there was thunder and lightning, and the rain became torrential.

The rain came down, down, down and the flood waters rose up, up, up. It rained for forty days and nights, until first the hills and then the mountains had disappeared, and as far as the eye could see there was nothing but water – and Noah's boat.

Looking after a boat-load of animals kept everyone busy. When the boat had been floating along for many days, Noah began to wonder what was going on outside. He opened a window and sent first a raven and then a dove to go and see. The raven flew off, but the dove came back because there was nowhere to land.

Noah started thinking that God had maybe forgotten them. But God had been watching over Noah's family and their precious cargo the whole time. Now a wind began to blow and, very slowly, the water started to go down.

When, seven days later, Noah let the dove fly away again, it came back with a sprig of olive leaves in its beak. It was proof that the land had begun to reappear.

Another week passed and, once more, Noah sent off the dove. But this time it did not come back because, at long last, the boat had come to rest on a mountain and the flood was over.

Then God told Noah that it was now time to leave the boat and begin a new life on earth.

The first thing that Noah did, once they were all back on dry land, was to build an altar and make a sacrifice to God in order to thank him for saving them.

In return, God promised that he would never again destroy the world with a flood. As a rainbow of dazzling colours appeared in the sky, God told Noah that this was a sign that he would always keep his promise.

4 God's Promise

Years passed after the great flood. One day, God spoke to a man named Abraham, who was descended from Noah's son, Shem.

'I want you to leave your country and your home,' God told him, 'and I will take you to a new land. Do as I tell you and I will bless you and make you famous. You will become the head of a great nation.'

As Abraham and his wife, Sarah, didn't have any children, he didn't see how this was possible, but he obeyed God and set out on his journey.

Many miles and many years later, Abraham was still travelling and still didn't have any children, so he began to doubt what God had told him. But one night, God repeated his promise. He told Abraham to look up at the night sky.

'Try and count all the stars that you can see,' said God, and Abraham gazed at the hundreds of thousands of stars shimmering in the darkness. 'That,' said God, 'is how many descendants you will have one day.'

Still more years passed until a day came when Abraham was sitting at the entrance of his tent and saw three men coming towards him. Running out to meet the strangers, he offered them food and drink and a chance to rest before going on with their journey.

It was the hottest part of the day and the men gladly accepted old Abraham's hospitality. So Sarah made a meal and Abraham served it to the visitors in the cool shade of a nearby tree.

Though Abraham and Sarah didn't know it, their guests were God and two of his heavenly servants.

'Where is your wife Sarah?' asked the visitors as they ate and drank. Abraham told them that she was inside the tent.

'In nine months' time,' said one of the men, 'Sarah will have a son.'

Now, Sarah was listening to this conversation from just inside the tent and she gave an angry laugh at the idea that she could ever become a mother. 'How ridiculous!' she said to herself. 'I am far too old now to have a baby! It's impossible.'

Sarah didn't think anyone could hear her, but the man called out and asked why she had laughed. 'I didn't,' said Sarah quickly, feeling suddenly embarrassed.

'Oh yes you did!' said the man. 'You said that it was impossible that you could have a baby. But tell me, Sarah, is *anything* really impossible for God?'

In that moment, Abraham and Sarah realized that it was God himself who was telling them this news.

The visitors went away. Nine months later, God's promise came true and Sarah gave birth to a baby boy. Abraham named him Isaac.

Holding her new baby, Sarah remembered how she had laughed in disbelief when she first heard the news and she laughed again, this time with happiness. 'God has given me such joy and laughter,' she said, 'and everyone who ever hears my story will laugh with me!'

5 JACOB AND ESAU

Abraham's son, Isaac, grew up and married Rebecca, and they had twin boys named Esau and Jacob. Even before they were born, it had felt to Rebecca as if her babies were fighting inside her, and God had told her that her boys would grow up to be rivals and that the younger one would turn out the stronger of the two.

The brothers could not have looked more different. Esau, who was born first, had a lot of thick red hair, while Jacob was smooth-skinned. They had little in common; Esau liked the outdoor life and enjoyed hunting, while Jacob preferred to stay at home. To make matters worse, Isaac made no secret of the fact that he preferred Esau, while Rebecca clearly loved Jacob best.

Eventually, things came to a head. Isaac had grown very old and didn't have long to live. One day, he asked Esau to go hunting and prepare a special meal for him. He promised that, after he had eaten it, he would give Esau his final blessing — something a father always passed on to his eldest son. Rebecca overheard this, and she and Jacob worked out a way to cheat Esau out of his blessing.

Jacob cooked a meal. Rebecca dressed him in his brother's best clothes and put pieces of goat's hair on his arms and his neck in case Isaac, who was almost blind, touched the boy and realized that he wasn't hairy like Esau.

While his brother was still out hunting, Jacob took the food to Isaac, who was surprised at how quick Esau had been.

'Which of my sons are you?' asked Isaac.

'Esau,' lied Jacob.

'Come closer,' said Isaac. 'Let me touch you.'

Jacob did so and the old man was very confused. 'Your voice *sounds* like Jacob's,' he said, 'but you *feel* like Esau. Are you *really* Esau?'

'I am,' said Jacob.

And so Isaac fell for the trick and gave the blessing meant for Esau to his younger son instead.

When Esau came home and discovered what his brother had done, he was so angry that he swore that, as soon as Isaac was dead, he would kill his brother.

Rebecca made Jacob run away. He settled down in a country called Haran, where he got married and started a family of his own. He worked hard but had many setbacks and was cheated by others just as he had cheated his own brother.

Years later, when Jacob had grown rich and had many herds of sheep, goats and camels, he decided to return to his own country.

Setting out, he wondered what would happen when he met his brother again. Would Esau still want to kill him?

One night, when Jacob was all alone thinking about his worries, a stranger suddenly jumped on him, grabbed hold and started wrestling with him.

The two men fought for hours, throwing each other this way and that but never once letting go. The stranger struck Jacob so hard that he knocked his hip out of joint, but even then Jacob wouldn't release his grip.

'Let me go!' shouted the stranger when it was almost dawn.

'I won't!' yelled Jacob, who was limping and in pain. 'Not unless you give me your blessing!'

'What is your name?' asked the man. And Jacob told him.

'Jacob,' said the man, 'you have struggled with people for many years, but tonight you have struggled with God!'

Only then did Jacob realize that it was God himself he had been wrestling with.

'Now,' said God, 'I am not only going to give you my blessing, I am going to give you a new name: from now on, Jacob, I am calling you Israel.'

And from then on, all the people who came from Jacob's family would be known as the people of Israel.

The next day, Jacob heard that Esau was on his way to meet him with 400 men. He was so frightened that he sent messengers on ahead with gifts of sheep, goats and cattle. But Jacob needn't have worried. Esau had done well in life too, and as soon as he saw his brother he ran up and kissed him. Both men were in tears as they hugged one another. At long last, the rivalry between them was over, and they were friends.

6 JOSEPH AND HIS COAT

Although Jacob had a large family, he loved his son Joseph more than all his other children. This made Joseph's brothers very jealous, especially when their father gave him an expensive coat, richly decorated in beautiful colours.

Then, one day, Joseph told his brothers that he had had a curious dream. 'We were out in the field, harvesting the wheat,' he said, 'when my bundle of wheat stood up straight and tall, and all your bundles bowed down to mine.'

Well, this made Joseph's brothers hate him all the more. 'Just who do you think you are?' they demanded. 'You may be Father's favourite, but you won't ever catch us bowing down to you!'

Not long after, when the brothers were off looking after the sheep and goats, Jacob sent Joseph on an errand to them.

The brothers saw Joseph coming and hatched a plot. 'Let's kill him,' they said, 'and throw his body in one of the old, dried-up wells. That will put paid to his dreams!'

The eldest brother, Reuben, didn't want Joseph to die. 'Don't kill him,' he begged the others, 'just throw him into the empty well and leave him there.'

The brothers eventually agreed. When Joseph arrived, they tore off his beautiful coat, ripped it to shreds and threw the boy down into the dark well.

There was no way to climb out but, although Joseph was scared, he believed that somehow God would help him.

Reuben was planning to go back later, haul Joseph out and send him home to Jacob. But while he was tending the goats, the other brothers pulled Joseph out of the well and sold him as a slave to a group of traders travelling to Egypt.

When Reuben found the well empty he was very distressed, but joined in with what the brothers did next. They killed a goat, smeared the blood on what was left of Joseph's coat and took it back to Jacob, telling him that Joseph had been killed by wild animals. When he heard this news, Jacob was heartbroken.

Meanwhile, the traders reached Egypt and sold Joseph to a man named Potiphar, who was captain of the guard in Pharaoh's palace.

Joseph worked hard, and Potiphar was so pleased with the young man that he made him his personal servant in charge of his house.

Everything went well until Potiphar's wife accused Joseph of something he hadn't done and Potiphar, believing his wife's lies, had Joseph arrested and thrown into prison.

Sometime later, Pharaoh's steward was sent to prison for offending the king. One night he had a strange dream that he didn't understand, but God showed Joseph the meaning and he told the steward that Pharaoh was going to forgive him and put him back in his job.

'When what I've told you comes true,' said Joseph, 'please tell Pharaoh that Joseph is in prison but has done nothing wrong.'

Everything happened just as Joseph had said, but the steward forgot all about him. Even so, God hadn't forgotten Joseph and had important plans for him.

7 JOSEPH AND THE FAMINE

Pharaoh was worried. He had had a strange dream that he didn't understand; when he asked his wise men and advisors what it meant, none of them could tell him.

Then his steward remembered how Joseph had explained his own dream when he was in prison, and suggested that Pharaoh ask the young man the meaning of the dream.

So Pharaoh sent for Joseph and described his dream: 'I saw seven cows come up out of the River Nile,' he said. 'They were fat and healthy. But soon afterwards, seven more cows came out of the river that were thin and scrawny, and they ate up the seven fat cows.'

God told Joseph the meaning of Pharaoh's dream. 'The seven fat cows,' he told the king, 'stand for seven years when the harvests will be the best Egypt has ever known. But these will be followed by seven years of terrible famine. Your Majesty needs to plan to store the extra food during the good years, so your people will not starve when the famine comes.'

The king agreed and was so impressed with Joseph that he made him governor of Egypt and put him in charge of carrying out the plan. Joseph was soon the most important man in the land after Pharaoh.

The seven years of wonderful harvests came and went, and the first year of famine left the people of Egypt without any crops. But, thanks to Joseph's plan, enough food had been stored away that no one went hungry.

The next year, the famine spread to all the countries around, and people began travelling to Egypt to buy corn to feed themselves and their animals.

Among those who came to buy supplies were the sons of Jacob. They arrived at the house of the governor of Egypt and, not recognizing him as their brother Joseph, they bowed down and begged his help.

Joseph's dream as a young man had come true, but he decided not to tell his brothers who he was. Pretending that he suspected them of being spies, he asked a lot of questions about their family. They told him that they had a younger brother, Benjamin, who had not come with them because their father hadn't let him out of his sight since another brother, called Joseph, had been killed.

Joseph gave his brothers the supplies they wanted but kept one of the brothers as a hostage and told them they had to return with their brother Benjamin to prove they had been telling the truth.

'This is all because of what we did to Joseph,' Reuben told his brothers as they set off for home.

When Jacob heard what had happened, he refused to let his sons take Benjamin to Egypt. But eventually, when their food began to run out, they had no choice but to take their young brother, go back and ask the governor for more supplies.

Joseph was really happy to see Benjamin again, but he still didn't tell the brothers who he was. He gave them food and rest, and sent them on their way with sacks filled with corn. But he hid a silver cup in Benjamin's sack.

Then, once they were on their way, Joseph's servants chased after them, searched their sacks and accused Benjamin of stealing Joseph's cup.

The terrified brothers returned to Egypt and begged the governor to let Benjamin go back to their father.

Unable to pretend any longer, Joseph burst into tears and told them who he really was.

The brothers were shocked, and ashamed of what they had done to Joseph.

'Don't blame yourselves,' he told them. 'God let you send me into Egypt so that I could save you all from the famine.'

Then Joseph sent his brothers home to fetch their father, who could scarcely believe the news, and the whole family travelled to Egypt where Pharaoh gave them the best land to live in and everything they needed.

8 SLAVES IN EGYPT

Joseph had become a great man while working for Pharaoh, but eventually they both grew old and died, and after many years a new king came to the Egyptian throne who knew nothing about Joseph or his people.

This pharaoh began worrying about the number of Israelites — Joseph's people — who were living in his country. He feared that one day they might form an army and go to war against the Egyptians.

So afraid was Pharaoh that he made the Israelites his slaves and forced them to work on building great cities. Then he did an even more terrible thing: he gave an order that any Israelite boys who were born should be thrown into the River Nile and drowned.

One Israelite woman, who had just had a lovely, healthy baby boy, decided that she was never going to let the Egyptians take him from her and kill him.

The mother made up her mind that somehow she was going to save him. So she hid him away in one of the rooms in the house. She or her daughter Miriam stayed close to him day and night, and were very careful to hush him whenever he started to cry.

Months passed, and the child was beginning to grow bigger. His mother realized that she wouldn't be able to keep him hidden for very much longer, but she didn't know what to do.

Then, when she was out working in the fields beside the River Nile with the other Israelite slaves, she noticed that every day a beautiful Egyptian princess – the daughter of Pharaoh – went down to the river near her father's palace to bathe.

This gave her an idea. She took an old basket and covered it with tar to make it watertight. Then she wrapped her baby up warm, put him in the basket and placed it among the tall reeds that grew in the water, where the princess was certain to find it.

Miriam watched to see what would happen. As the princess was bathing, she suddenly heard the sound of a baby crying and, searching among the reeds, found the basket and its contents.

The princess realized that this child had somehow managed to survive her father's plan to kill all Israelite baby boys. Feeling sorry for the baby, she announced that she was going to take care of him.

At that moment, Miriam ran up. 'If you like,' she cleverly

suggested, 'I could find you an Israelite woman who could nurse the baby for you.'

When the princess agreed, Miriam went to fetch her own mother, who was so happy to have not only saved her baby's life, but also to be able to look after him as he grew up.

The princess gave the child a name that, thousands of years later, is known throughout the world.

She called him Moses.

9 THE BURNING BUSH

The boy Moses grew up in Pharaoh's palace and was educated as if he had been a prince of Egypt, but he never forgot that he had been born an Israelite.

Moses hated how the Egyptians treated his own people. One day, when he saw an Egyptian kill an Israelite slave, he did something terrible: thinking that nobody was watching, he killed the Egyptian and hid the body in the sand.

The next day, Moses saw two Israelites fighting one another and tried to stop them. 'Isn't it bad enough that the Egyptians beat you up,' he shouted, 'without beating each other up as well?'

One of the men turned on Moses. 'What are you going to do about it?' he asked. 'Kill us like you killed that Egyptian yesterday?'

This made Moses afraid, so he ran away and hid in a land called Midian, where he became a shepherd.

Years passed and Pharaoh died, but the next king of Egypt continued to treat the Israelites as cruelly as before.

One day, when Moses was out in the mountains looking after the goats, he saw a strange sight. There, right in front of him, was a bush on fire. Amazingly, even though the flames leaped and raged, the bush didn't burn up.

Moses was about to take a closer look when a voice suddenly spoke to him from the bush.

'Moses,' said the voice, 'do not come any nearer! Take off your sandals! I am God, and you are standing on holy ground!'

Taking off his sandals, Moses knelt down in front of the blazing bush.

'Listen!' said God. 'I have seen how cruelly the Egyptians treat my people and I am sending you to Pharaoh to tell him to let them go free.'

'How am I going to do that?' asked Moses. 'I am nobody!'

'I will be with you,' replied God. 'You will lead my people out of slavery and bring them here to worship me on this very mountain.'

Moses had another question. 'The people will ask who sent me. What am I supposed to tell them?'

'Tell them,' said God, 'that you have been sent by the God of Abraham, Isaac and Jacob!'

Moses was still worried. 'But what if no one believes me?'

'What are you holding in your hand?' God asked.

'It's just my staff,' said Moses, 'the stick I use when I'm walking with the goats.'

'Throw it on the ground!' said God.

So Moses did and, immediately, it turned into a snake. Moses jumped out of the way.

'Now pick it up by the tail!' said God.

Nervously, Moses bent down and picked up the snake. As he did so, it was a stick once more.

'Do this,' God told him, 'to prove to people that I have sent you.'

Again Moses hesitated. 'I am a very poor speaker – no one will take any notice of me…'

'Find your brother Aaron and take him with you,' said God. 'Now, go! I will be with you both and I will tell you what to say.'

10 OUT OF EGYPT

God sent Moses and Aaron to tell Pharaoh to release the Israelite people from slavery and allow them to leave Egypt.

To show Pharaoh that God was with them, Aaron threw down the staff he leaned on when walking and, as had happened with Moses' stick, it turned into a snake.

Pharaoh called for his magicians and they used trickery to make their sticks into snakes as well. Aaron's snake immediately swallowed up all the others, but still Pharaoh refused to release the Israelites. So Moses told him, 'God will show you that he must be obeyed! Terrible things will happen to your people because you refuse.'

The next day, Moses and Aaron met Pharaoh as he was walking beside the Nile. Taking his stick, Aaron hit the surface of the water and, suddenly, it turned into a river of blood so that the Egyptians had no water to drink.

Even then, Pharaoh wouldn't let the Israelites leave his land, so God went on causing disasters to happen to the Egyptians.

A great plague of frogs came crawling out of the river by the thousand and went hopping and leaping into everyone's houses, including the royal palace. Then great swarms of stinging gnats and biting flies brought the country to a standstill, and then came diseases that made the Egyptians ill and killed all their animals.

Each time, Pharaoh pretended that he would release the Israelites but, as soon as God took each plague away, he changed his mind.

So the Egyptians' troubles went on. A violent hail storm flattened and ruined the crops, and a plague of locusts swept through the land like a great cloud, with the insects eating up all the plants that had not been destroyed in the storm. And then, for three days, there was total darkness over the whole of Egypt.

When, despite everything, Pharaoh still wouldn't let the Israelites go free, God told Moses, 'I will punish the Egyptians one more time and after that you will leave. At midnight I will pass through this land, and when I do so, the eldest son of every Egyptian family will die.'

God told Moses that the Israelite people were to kill a lamb or goat to make a meal and paint some of the animal's blood on the doorposts of their houses.

'When I see the blood on your doorposts,' God told Moses, 'I will pass over, and no Israelite children will die.'

Then God told Moses how his people were to prepare their last meal in Egypt. Everyone was to eat it with their shoes on and their possessions packed, so as to be ready to leave.

This was the beginning of the feast, still celebrated today, called Passover.

At midnight, all of Egypt was filled with the sound of people crying and sobbing as the firstborn son of every family died — from Pharaoh's son to the child of the slave who made the king's bread.

Only then did Pharaoh send for Moses and Aaron and, at long last, tell them to take the people and go.

Day and night, God led the Israelites through the desert until they came to the edge of the Red Sea.

Meanwhile, Pharaoh had changed his mind yet again, and when the people looked back, they saw that Pharaoh and the entire Egyptian army were chasing after them. The people were now trapped between their enemy and the sea.

But God told Moses to lift his staff up over the water. And as he did so, the sea parted in the middle and rolled back on each side until it was like two great walls of water with a way through between for the Israelite people to reach the other shore.

Just as the last of the Israelites reached dry land, Pharaoh's army swarmed in after them. But while they were still crossing, God made the sea roll back in again, drowning the Egyptians in a great torrent of water.

As the Israelite people watched their enemy being swept away on the flood, they realized just how powerful God was and how he had used Moses to lead them to safety and freedom.

11 Ten Commandments

Once the Israelites had escaped from Pharaoh's army and crossed the Red Sea to safety, God led his people across the desert, giving them food and water whenever they were hungry and thirsty, and protecting them from their enemies.

Eventually they came to a mountain called Sinai, which was the place where God had first spoken to Moses in the burning bush. Now God told Moses that the people were to prepare for a special encounter.

A mass of black cloud settled on the top of the mountain. There was thunder and lightning, and the Israelites standing at the bottom were so afraid that they trembled.

Moses went up to the very top of the mountain and there God told him the laws that he wanted his people to keep.

There were ten important truths about how everybody should behave and their responsibilities – first of all to God and then to each other.

Remember that it was God who rescued you from slavery in Egypt. He is the only God you should love and serve.

Do not make a god of anything that exists in heaven and earth.

Respect God's name and do not misuse it in any way.

Set one day of the week aside and keep it as a special day of rest.

Treat your parents with love and respect.

Do not commit murder.

Do not be unfaithful in marriage.

Do not steal anything that does not belong to you.

Do not lie about people or accuse them of things they have not done.

Do not be jealous or envious of the things that another person owns.

As well as these ten laws – or commandments – God gave Moses many other rules that he wanted his people to follow.

God said that they were to be fair and honest and not spread lies or rumours. No one was ever to accept a bribe and everyone was to have a right to justice.

God also wanted people to be good to each other and to help one another. They were to take care of the wives and children of any man who died and to be kind to foreigners because they had themselves been foreigners when they were slaves in Egypt.

To remind his people that these were important and lasting truths, God carved his Ten Commandments on stone, and Moses brought them down from the mountain and gave them to the Israelites.

Then Moses asked if the people were willing to make a promise to God to keep these laws, and they all agreed.

This agreement between God and his people was called the covenant: God would be their God; they would be God's people. To seal the promise, Moses built an altar and offered a sacrifice.

On that day, the people made a pledge. 'We will obey God,' they said, 'and do everything that he has asked.'

God then told Moses how the pieces of stone with his laws on were to be looked after. They were to be placed in a special box that was to be called the covenant box – and this was to be guarded and cared for by priests and to travel with the Israelites wherever they went.

Whenever they stopped on their journeys, the priests were to put up a tabernacle, or tent, in which the covenant box was to be kept. This was to be God's house – the place where he would live among his people.

12 THE WALLS OF JERICHO

Moses grew old and, knowing that he was going to die, he asked God to find someone to lead the people of Israel after he was gone. God told him to choose a man named Joshua.

After Moses died, God gave orders to Joshua: 'The time has come,' he said, 'for my people to go into the land of Canaan that I promised them. You must be sure of yourself and strong-minded. You must never be afraid, because I will be with you wherever you go.'

Joshua told the Israelites what God had said, and the people promised to follow Joshua and obey God.

The first thing Joshua did was to send out spies to explore the land of Canaan and find out what difficulties lay ahead – especially in the city of Jericho, which was surrounded by great, high, thick walls.

Joshua's spies went into Jericho and stayed with a woman named Rahab, who had a house built into the city wall; but the news reached the king of Jericho, and he sent his guards to arrest them.

Because Rahab believed in the things she had heard about the God of the Israelites, she hid the spies and told the guards that the men had already left the city.

While the guards were searching the roads for miles around, Rahab helped the spies escape using a rope lowered from her window in the city wall. In return, the spies promised that Rahab and her family would be safe when Joshua's army invaded Jericho.

The spies returned to Joshua and, armed with the information they had brought back, the Israelites set out for Jericho. While they were on the way, Joshua suddenly saw a man standing in front of him, holding a sword.

'Are you one of our soldiers?' asked Joshua. 'Or are you one of the enemy?'

'I am neither,' replied the man. 'I am the commander of the army of God!'

Joshua fell to his knees and said, 'Please, sir, tell me what I am to do.'

The heavenly messenger explained God's orders, and Joshua called the people together and told them the plan.

The priests were to march around the city walls carrying the covenant box and blowing trumpets, while the people were to follow in silence.

So, just as they had been told, the Israelites marched around Jericho and then returned to their camp.

They did the same thing the next day and the day after that. For six days, the Israelites blew their trumpets and marched around the walls of Jericho, but nothing happened.

On the seventh day, however, Joshua's army marched round the walls, not once, but seven times. And on the seventh time around, as the priests were about to blow their trumpets, Joshua told the people to shout at the top of their voices and the city of Jericho would be theirs.

So the trumpets rang out loud and clear, and all the people yelled and shouted.

Then, all of a sudden, there came another sound: a tremendous, ear-splitting sound as the great thick walls began to crack and break, and the towers and battlements shook, and the whole city toppled and crumbled to the ground in a mountain of rubble and dust.

God had kept his promise to give the city of Jericho to his people, and they in turn kept their promise and made sure that no harm came to Rahab and her family.

13 ACHAN'S CRIME

After Jericho had been defeated, Joshua gave strict orders from God that the city and everything in it had to be treated as an offering to God and that the Israelites were not to keep back anything that they found in the city for themselves.

Everybody did as Joshua said, except one man, named Achan, who disobeyed God's order.

Not long after the battle of Jericho, Joshua sent spies out again to see if they could capture another city called Ai. The spies returned to say that the Israelites could easily attack and defeat it with just a small part of their army.

So 3,000 men marched to Ai, but the people who lived there beat them off and the Israelites lost their courage and ran away.

Joshua threw himself on the ground in front of the covenant box and called out to God. 'Everyone will hear of this defeat,' he cried, 'and they will attack us and kill us! Why has this happened?'

'Because,' God said, 'someone among my people has disobeyed me by taking things from Jericho and keeping them for themselves.'

The next day, Joshua called all the people before him tribe by tribe, family by family and then finally one by one until he discovered that the person who had disobeyed God was Achan.

'What have you to say for yourself?' asked Joshua. 'Tell me the truth.'

'It's all my fault!' said Achan. 'I found a beautiful cloak and wanted it for myself, so I stole it and hid it in my tent with some silver and a bar of gold. I didn't think anyone would know, but I see now that I couldn't hide what I had done from God!'

Achan was punished for his disobedience and God forgave the people of Israel.

Soon afterwards, the Israelites captured the city of Ai and went on to defeat many other enemies. And then, just as God had meant them to do, they settled and made their homes in the land he had given them.

14 THE STORY OF RUTH

There was a time when a terrible famine hit Israel. A man named Elimelech, along with his wife Naomi and their two sons, left his home in Bethlehem and went on a long journey to live in the country of Moab.

While they were there Elimelech died, leaving Naomi a widow with her two boys, who had grown up and married local girls. Then, a few years later, there was more sadness for Naomi when both her sons died, leaving her alone with her daughters-in-law, Orpah and Ruth.

The famine in Israel was now over and Naomi decided to return to Bethlehem to be near her relatives. Orpah and Ruth set out to go with her, but when they had gone a little way, Naomi kissed the young women goodbye and tried to send them back. 'I'm going to my old home,' she told them. 'You should stay near *your* home. You will find new husbands and get married again.'

Orpah and Ruth both cried and argued with Naomi. Orpah finally agreed to go back, but Ruth insisted on going with Naomi. 'Please don't make me leave you!' she begged. 'Wherever you go, I will go; wherever you live, I will live. Your people will be my people and your God will be my God. Nothing but death will separate me from you!'

Back in Bethlehem, life was hard for the two women, but Ruth went to work in the cornfields, gathering up the grain that was left behind by the people harvesting the crops.

The owner of the fields was a rich man named Boaz, who was a relative of Naomi's husband. When he heard how Ruth had left her own home and family to take care of her mother-in-law, he decided to help her.

Boaz invited her to eat with him and secretly told the workers who took care of his fields to make sure that she was looked after.

'I know how kind you've been to Naomi,' he told Ruth, 'and I pray that God will reward you for what you have done.'

'Thank you, sir,' replied Ruth. 'You are very kind to me.'

Boaz told his workers that not only were they to allow Ruth to pick up the corn that was left behind in the harvest, but they were also to leave some especially for her to find.

Ruth worked in Boaz's fields throughout the harvest time. When the men were beating the grain out of the corn, Naomi sent Ruth to Boaz to remind him that they were relatives and to ask if he would make her his wife.

'Will you marry me?' asked Ruth. 'Naomi and I would then be part of a family again.'

Boaz looked at Ruth and smiled. 'Yes,' he said. 'You could have gone anywhere and found a younger or richer husband for yourself than me, but you have been true to Naomi and I will be true to you!'

So, Ruth and Boaz were married and had a son named Obed, who, when he grew up, became the grandfather of David, Israel's greatest king.

15 THE BOY SAMUEL

There was a woman named Hannah, who desperately wanted to have a baby. One day, she went into God's house and prayed long and hard that she might have a child.

Eli, the old priest, watched the woman for a long, long time; because she spent so much time saying her prayers, he began to wonder if there was something wrong.

Hannah explained what she had been asking God to do for her and how she had told God that if he answered her prayer and gave her a son, then she would give him back to God to work in the place of worship.

The old priest smiled at Hannah and said, 'May the God of Israel give you what you have asked him for.'

And God *did* answer Hannah's prayer and gave her a baby boy whom she named Samuel.

After a few years, when Samuel was old enough, Hannah took him to Eli. The priest remembered

Hannah and agreed that Samuel could help him with his work in God's house.

Eli also had two sons who were priests, but they did not obey God's laws about how priests were to behave. People complained to Eli, but he was old, tired and nearly blind and he did nothing about it.

One night, when Samuel was lying asleep in the part of God's house where the covenant box was kept, he woke to hear a voice calling his name. 'Samuel! Samuel!'

'Yes, sir!' he answered. Thinking it was Eli, he ran to where the old priest was sleeping and said, 'Here I am! You called me.'

'I didn't call you,' replied Eli. 'You were probably dreaming. Now go back to bed.'

Samuel did as he was told, but not long afterwards, he heard the voice again, calling, 'Samuel! Samuel!'

For a second time, the boy ran to Eli and asked him why he had called; for a second time, Eli sent the boy back to bed.

When Samuel ran to Eli a third time, the old priest realized that it was God who was calling to the boy, so he told him, 'If you hear the voice again, say, "Speak, Lord, your servant is listening."'

Samuel went back to his bed, and when he heard the voice a fourth time, he was ready. 'Samuel!' called the voice and, just as Eli had told him, Samuel replied, 'Speak, Lord, your servant is listening.'

Then God spoke to Samuel and told him that he was going to punish Eli's sons for all the wrong things they had been doing. Samuel listened to everything God said and then went back to sleep.

The next morning, Eli asked Samuel what God had said to him, but the boy was afraid to pass on God's message. 'Tell me!' said Eli. 'Don't keep anything from me.'

So Samuel told Eli what God had told him and the priest knew that what the boy had said would come true. He also knew that because Samuel had listened to God and had obeyed him, he would grow up to be a true servant of God.

That is exactly what happened, and when Samuel became a man, God chose him to appoint the first kings to rule over the people of Israel.

16 DAVID AND GOLIATH

There was a time when Saul was the king of the Israelites and the people were at war with the Philistines. Among Saul's army were three sons of a man named Jesse who lived in Bethlehem. Jesse's youngest son, David, spent his time in the hills taking care of his father's sheep.

One day, Jesse told David to take some supplies to his brothers. When the boy reached the Israelites' camp, he found that the king's army was lined up and ready to face the enemy.

David ran to find his brothers and, just as he reached the front line, a towering giant of a man stepped forward from the Philistine army. He was covered in bronze armour that flashed in the sun and he carried a long, heavy spear. In a loud, deep voice that echoed around the hills, he issued a challenge to Saul's men.

'I am Goliath!' he bellowed. 'Choose one of your men to fight me. If he wins and kills me, the Philistines will be your slaves, but if I win, you will be our slaves. So come on. Pick someone and let's fight.'

Saul's army was terrified, but young David asked the soldiers what reward the king would give to the man who beat Goliath. The men told the boy that the king had promised that anyone who defeated Goliath would marry his daughter.

One of David's brothers overheard the conversation. 'What are you doing here?' he asked. 'Why aren't you at home looking after the sheep?'

'I only asked a question!' replied David. 'I'd be willing to fight Goliath if no one else will do it.' His brothers laughed, but someone told King Saul and he sent for David.

'Your Majesty,' said David bravely, 'let me go and deal with this man!'

'No!' King Saul replied. 'How could you ever fight Goliath?'

'I take care of my father's sheep,' David told the king, 'and I've fought and killed lions and bears that have attacked the flock. I'll do the same with this man who has dared to challenge the army of God's people.'

'You're just a boy,' said the king, 'and Goliath has been a soldier all his life!'

'God protected me when I faced those lions and bears,' David replied, 'and he will look after me now.'

So the king agreed and gave David his own armour to wear, but it was so heavy that the boy could hardly walk.

'I can't fight in all of this,' said David, and

58

taking off the armour he picked up his shepherd's stick and walked out to meet the giant.

David was carrying a slingshot and on the way, as he crossed a stream, he picked up five smooth pebbles and put them in his bag.

Goliath stood waiting with his shield and spear and sword at the ready. As soon as he saw David approaching, he gave a great roar of laughter. 'What have you got a stick for?' he jeered. 'Do you think I'm a dog and that you can beat me with that?'

David kept walking towards Goliath, and the big man's laughter turned to fierce anger. 'Come on, then, boy!' he yelled. 'Come and fight me and let me give your dead body to the birds and the animals to eat!'

David went on walking. 'You have your armour and shield to protect you,' he called out, 'and a sword and a spear to fight with. But I have God on my side and when I beat you, everyone will see that he is all-powerful.'

Goliath snarled and raised his spear, but David slipped his hand into his bag, grabbed a stone, put it into his slingshot and aimed it at Goliath.

Before the giant could hurl his spear, the stone hit him in the middle of the forehead and he dropped down dead.

As soon as their hero fell, the Philistine army turned and ran away.

Saul rewarded David and made him an officer in his army; years later, he would become one of the greatest of all the kings of Israel.

17 WISE KING SOLOMON

When King David died, after ruling for forty years, his son Solomon came to the throne.

Being young and feeling unprepared for the responsibility, Solomon prayed to God to give him help. 'What would you like me to give you?' asked God. Solomon told God that he wanted to be wise.

God was pleased. 'You could have asked for a long life,' he said, 'or great riches, but because you have asked me for wisdom I will make you wiser than any man has ever been and give you more honour and wealth than any other king.'

A few days later, two women came to see King Solomon to ask him to settle an argument between them.

'We live in the same house,' said the first woman, 'and we both gave birth to baby boys around the same time. The other night, this other woman's baby died, and while I was asleep she switched it for mine, pretending that my son is her child and leaving me with the dead baby.'

'It *is* my child!' yelled the other woman. 'The dead child is hers.'

'No!' shouted the first woman. 'The living child is mine.'

Then King Solomon spoke. 'You both say that the living child is yours,' he said, 'and that the dead child belongs to the other one. So I shall have to decide what is to be done.'

Solomon thought a moment and then sent for one of his guards.

'Draw your sword!' ordered the king. 'Cut the child in two and give the women half each.'

The guard grabbed the child and raised his sword above his head. As he did so, the first woman screamed and threw herself at the king's feet. 'No, please!' she begged. 'Don't kill the child! Give it to her, if you must, but please, let the boy live!'

'Put away your sword,' the king told the guard, 'and give the child to this woman. She would have given him away rather than let him die, so she is the real mother.'

Solomon had asked for wisdom and he knew now that God had given it to him.

18 Fire from Heaven

King Solomon built a great temple in Jerusalem for the worship of God. It was made of the finest materials, and inside was placed the covenant box, containing the laws given to Moses.

But the years passed and, after Solomon died, the people were divided into north and south. Other kings came and went who began to forget what God had done for his people and the promises they had made to him.

One of these rulers, King Ahab in the north, had a queen named Jezebel, who believed in a god called Baal. Jezebel persuaded her husband to make the Israelites worship Baal, and the people were too scared to disobey the king.

Someone who was *not* scared was a man named Elijah, who followed the true God and decided to prove to everyone that Baal was not a real god at all.

Elijah issued a challenge for King Ahab, the 450 priests who served Baal and all the people to meet him at a mountain called Carmel.

Two bulls were killed and were placed on bundles of wood on altars so that they could be offered as a burned sacrifice to the two gods.

'Neither of us will light the fire,' Elijah told the priests. 'You can pray to Baal to send fire and I will pray to God, and we'll see who answers. I'm outnumbered 450 to one, but I'll let you try first!'

The priests of Baal prayed and prayed; they jumped and they danced and ran about shouting and screaming, 'Answer us, Baal! Send down fire!' But nothing happened.

Elijah made fun of the priests. 'You had better pray louder!' he said. 'I think Baal is asleep. Or maybe he's gone on a journey somewhere!'

After several more hours, there was still no fire to light Baal's sacrifice. 'Now,' said Elijah, 'let us see what my God can do!'

Elijah dug a deep trench all round his altar. And then he gave orders for jars of water to be emptied over the sacrifice and the wood; this was done three times until everything was soaking wet and the water that had run down had filled the trench to the brim.

When all that had been done, Elijah began praying to God. 'Lord God of Abraham, Isaac and Jacob!' he called. 'Prove now that you are the God of Israel and that I am your servant!'

Everyone was waiting and wondering what would happen. 'Answer me!' prayed Elijah. 'Show the people that you are their God and that you want them to go back to loving and serving you!'

In that moment, there was a great rush and a roar. Fire poured down from the sky, setting the wet wood alight, burning up the sacrifice, scorching all the earth and drying up the water in the trench.

God had spoken, and the terrified Israelites threw themselves on the ground. 'The Lord is God!' they called out. 'The Lord alone is God!'

19 Naaman the Proud

The Israelites had fought many battles with other people, including the Syrians, whose army was led by a commanding officer called Naaman.

He was a great soldier, but he suffered from a terrible skin disease that no one knew how to cure.

Naaman's wife had an Israelite slave girl. She told her mistress that she knew of a wise man in her country, named Elisha, who could make her master well again.

When Naaman heard this, he told the king of Syria and, as the two lands were not at war at the time, the king sent Naaman to the king of Israel with gifts and a letter asking for him to be made better.

When the king of Israel read the letter, he was very upset and sent for Elisha. 'How does the king of Syria expect me to cure this man?' he asked. 'Does he think that I am God? He's trying to pick a fight with me so that we will go to war again!'

'Don't worry,' replied Elisha. 'Send the man to me!'

When Naaman arrived at Elisha's house in a horse-drawn chariot, a servant came out to say that Naaman was to wash himself seven times in the River Jordan and the disease would be gone.

But Naaman was a proud man. 'You insult me!' he said. 'There are plenty of better rivers where I could bathe in my own country.' He was just about to ride off in anger when one of his servants said, 'If you'd been told to do something really difficult, you would have done it. Why not do this simple thing and see if you're made well?'

Naaman thought this over and finally agreed. He went to the River Jordan and washed seven times, and when he came out of the water, the disease had vanished and his skin was completely healthy.

Overjoyed, Naaman rushed back to Elisha to thank him. 'I know now that there is only one god,' he said, 'and that is the God of Israel, who has made me well. I must return to my own people, but I will only ever serve and honour your God!'

20 Jerusalem at War

When Hezekiah was king of Judah in the south, the Assyrians continued to make war on other nations in order to expand their empire. They defeated several of Judah's fortified cities. All too soon, the emperor of Assyria, Sennacherib, was planning an attack on Jerusalem itself.

King Hezekiah did everything he could to protect the city. He gave orders for it to be made safer: an outer wall was built and the inner walls were repaired and strengthened with new towers built on top of them.

Then the king sent men out into the surrounding countryside to block up all the wells so that there wouldn't be any fresh water supplies when the enemy began to get close to Jerusalem. At the same time, he had a tunnel dug to bring fresh water into the city.

A great many spears and shields were made and the men of Jerusalem were formed into an army. When all these preparations had been made, King Hezekiah spoke to the people and told them to be brave. 'Don't be afraid of the Assyrian emperor and his army,' he said. 'They only have human powers, but we have the power of God to help us and to fight our battles!'

But Sennacherib sent a messenger with a letter to King Hezekiah. 'The god you are trusting in won't help you,' read the letter. 'Do you think you can escape? Do you really believe that words will help you against our great military strength?'

The king was afraid and took the letter into God's Temple to ask for help. 'Do you see what is happening to us?' he prayed. 'Sennacherib insults you and threatens your people. We believe and trust in you – please save us from our enemies!'

A wise man named Isaiah, who received messages from God, told King Hezekiah that his prayer had been heard and that God had promised to protect Jerusalem and his people.

That very night, one of God's heavenly messengers attacked the enemy camp. In the morning, thousands of the Assyrian troops were dead; Sennacherib gave up his plans to invade Jerusalem and went back to his own country.

21 GOOD KING JOSIAH

Again and again, the Israelites forgot their promises to God and, by the time Josiah became king, the great temple that Solomon had built in Jerusalem was no longer being properly looked after.

So Josiah ordered builders and carpenters to be put to work so that the Temple could be repaired. While this was being done, one of the priests discovered an old book containing the commandments that God had given to Moses.

The priest took the book to the king and when Josiah read it he was shocked and afraid because he realized that the people had not been obeying God's laws.

'This is terrible!' he cried in tears. 'We have stopped doing the things that God told us to do and we've been doing many other things that he told us *not* to do. Worst of all, we have been worshipping and offering sacrifices to gods that are not the one true God!'

As soon as he had understood the truth, the king called all the leaders of the people to a meeting in the Temple and he read them what it said in the book.

Then, in front of all the people, Josiah made a promise to God. 'From now on,' he said, 'I will keep all God's laws and do all those things that he has told us to do.' And all the Israelites promised to do the same.

On the king's orders, the statues and idols to other gods that were in Jerusalem and all the cities of Judah were knocked down, chopped up, broken into bits and burned on great, blazing bonfires.

Then, for the first time in many years, the Israelites celebrated the Passover. This was the festival that God had told his people to hold every year as a reminder of the last meal that the Israelites had eaten on the night before God had freed them from slavery and led them to a new land.

22 Jonah and the Fish

This is the story of Jonah, a man who was chosen by God to do a job that he really didn't want to do.

God told Jonah that he was to go to the city of Nineveh and to tell the Assyrians who lived there that he had seen all the wrong things they were doing – and that if they didn't stop, they would be punished.

Now, Assyria was the sworn enemy of Israel, and Jonah didn't want to take them God's message. 'I know what will happen,' he thought. 'The people of Nineveh will change their ways and God will forgive them!'

Jonah decided to go as far away from Nineveh as he possibly could, so he travelled to a town by the sea called Joppa and booked a place on board a ship heading for Spain.

The journey had scarcely begun when God stirred up a great storm at sea. Rain lashed down and the wind whipped up the waves and tossed the ship this way and that until it was about to capsize. The sailors panicked and started throwing the ship's cargo overboard and calling out for help to the various gods they believed in, shouting as loud as they could in the hope of being heard above the roaring of the wind and the waves.

Somehow, Jonah managed to sleep through the storm until the captain found him down in the hold of the ship and woke him. 'Get up!' he yelled. 'Pray to your god and maybe he will help us and let us live!'

Jonah knew at once what had happened – and it wasn't long before the other sailors knew, too.

When the storm showed no sign of easing up, the men decided to draw straws, believing that it would show them who was to blame for the danger they were all in. Jonah was not surprised when he was left holding the short straw.

'Who are you?' the sailors asked. 'What have you done to bring us such bad luck?'

'I am an Israelite,' Jonah told them, 'and I am running away from God.'

'What can we do?' the captain asked. 'Is there any way to stop the storm?'

'Yes,' replied Jonah. 'This is all my fault. Throw me overboard and the storm will end.'

The sailors didn't want to do this, so they struggled on, trying hard to get the ship to shore. But it was no good. There was nothing to be done. So, praying to God to forgive them, they took Jonah and threw him over the side of the ship. All at once, the storm died down and the sea became calm.

Down, down, down into the sea sank Jonah. Just when it seemed that he was going to drown, God sent a large fish to swallow him up.

Jonah lived inside the fish for three days and nights, and during that time he thought about what he had done. He told God that he had been wrong, that he was sorry for having disobeyed him, and he thanked him for saving his life.

So God made the big fish cough Jonah up onto a beach and then he told him a second time to go to Nineveh.

Jonah set off without delay. When he reached the city, he told everyone that God had seen all the wrong things they were doing.

'In forty days,' said Jonah in a terrible voice, 'Nineveh will be wiped off the face of the earth!'

The people of Nineveh believed Jonah's message and all of them, from the king down to the poorest family, gave up eating food and prayed day and night in the hope that God would forgive them.

And when God saw that they had changed their ways, he did not destroy Nineveh.

Jonah got really angry. 'This is exactly what I knew would happen!' he told God. 'These Assyrians don't deserve to be forgiven. They deserve to die!'

But now it was Jonah's turn to be taught a lesson.

'What right have you to be so angry?' asked God. 'I am God. I created everyone and everything that is in the world and have every right to care for them and to show them love and forgiveness.'

23 The Fiery Furnace

There was a time when Jerusalem was attacked by the Babylonian king, Nebuchadnezzar, and his army. Many treasures were stolen from God's Temple and several young men were taken prisoner and carried off to act as servants to the king.

Three of the Israelite prisoners were given new names –

Shadrach, Meshach and Abednego – and they were taught to read and write the language of the Babylonians. After three years of studying, they joined King Nebuchadnezzar's royal court and impressed him with their great knowledge and wisdom.

Eventually, Nebuchadnezzar put Shadrach, Meshach and Abednego in charge of a part of his kingdom. But some of the Babylonians were jealous of the Israelites and began to look for an opportunity to get them into trouble.

Their chance came when the king made a great gold statue of the god he believed in and ordered that everyone had to bow down and worship it; anyone who refused would be thrown into a blazing, fiery furnace.

The jealous Babylonians told the king that Shadrach, Meshach and Abednego had disobeyed this order because it was against one of the laws of their God.

This made Nebuchadnezzar very angry, and he sent for the three men. 'Is it true what I hear?' he shouted. 'They say you do not bow down and worship the statue of my god! Do you know what will happen to you because you have refused?'

'Your Majesty,' replied Shadrach, Meshach and Abednego, 'if the God we believe in is able to save us from the flames of your furnace, then he will. But whatever happens, there is no way that we can bow down and worship your golden statue.'

'Take them away!' screamed Nebuchadnezzar in a fury. 'Heat the furnace until it is hotter than the hottest it has ever been! Then when the flames are at their height, tie up Shadrach, Meshach and Abednego and throw them in. I shall watch them burn for their disobedience.'

The furnace was heated until it was seven times hotter than usual. Then the strongest men in Nebuchadnezzar's army tied up Shadrach, Meshach and Abednego with thick ropes and hurled them into the fiercely roaring flames.

As the king watched, waiting to see the three men burned to death, something amazing happened. Nebuchadnezzar suddenly saw Shadrach, Meshach and Abednego, untied and walking around unhurt among the leaping flames with a fourth person, who shone brighter than the fire itself and who was a messenger of God.

The king rushed to the door of the furnace. 'Shadrach, Meshach and Abednego!' he shouted. 'Come out of the fire!'

The three Israelites walked out of the flames without a single burn and without even the smell of smoke on their clothes.

'These men,' said the king, 'disobeyed my order and risked their lives rather than worship a god other than their own – and he has saved them! Today, I give a new order that Shadrach, Meshach and Abednego are to be respected by all men because the God they believe in is the greatest of all gods.'

24 Daniel and the Lions

Another of the Israelites who was taken prisoner when Nebuchadnezzar attacked Jerusalem was Daniel and, like Shadrach, Meshach and Abednego, he became a trusted servant of the king.

Daniel eventually became Nebuchadnezzar's chief advisor and served as a member of the royal court through the reigns of several kings.

When Darius became king of the empire, he appointed Daniel and two other men to be supervisors responsible for making sure that everything was done according to the king's laws. When Daniel did the job better than the others, Darius decided to promote him and put him in charge of his entire kingdom.

The other supervisors were not pleased and started plotting to get rid of Daniel. So they convinced King Darius to make a new law saying that for thirty days no one was allowed to ask for anything from any god or any human being other than the king himself. This law was to be strictly kept, and anyone who didn't keep it was to be thrown into a pit filled with lions.

When Daniel heard that the king had signed this law, he went home and, as he did three times every day, knelt down at a window in his house that faced towards his home city of Jerusalem and prayed to God.

Daniel's enemies saw him and went to King Darius. 'Daniel has broken your law,' they said. 'He's guilty and must be thrown to the lions!'

The king was terribly upset: he liked and trusted Daniel and didn't want anything to happen to him, so he put off ordering his execution, hoping to find some way round the law. But at the end of the day, the men returned and told the king that he had to pass sentence on Daniel. 'The law is the law,' they said. 'Your Majesty has no choice!'

Then Darius had to give the order for Daniel to be put into the pit with the lions. The king said to Daniel, 'I hope and pray that the God you serve so faithfully will rescue you.'

A stone was rolled across the opening to the pit and it was sealed so that no one could rescue Daniel. There were roars and snarls and then silence.

The king spent the night without food or sleep, pacing to and fro in his palace and worrying about what had happened to Daniel.

As soon as it was light, Darius rushed to the lion pit and called out, 'Daniel! Are you alive? Did your God save you from the lions?' He waited anxiously and then heard Daniel calling out. 'Yes,' he said, 'I am alive! God kept me safe because I am innocent and have done nothing wrong against Your Majesty.'

King Darius was overjoyed; he had the stone rolled away and, to everyone's surprise, there was Daniel sitting among the lions as if they were tame animals.

Daniel was pulled out of the pit and his enemies were arrested and punished by the king. Then Darius issued a proclamation: 'Everyone is to respect Daniel's God because he is a living God who saves and rescues and will rule forever.'

25 Rebuilding God's City

Nehemiah was an Israelite who worked for the emperor of Persia, Artaxerxes. He was made very sad when he heard reports that the walls of Jerusalem were once again broken down and the city of his people was falling into ruin.

Noticing that Nehemiah was unhappy, the emperor wanted to know what was wrong; when he heard the reason, he asked Nehemiah what he wanted to do.

'I want to go and rebuild Jerusalem,' Nehemiah replied. The emperor not only gave him permission but sent some of his soldiers with him and letters to the keeper of the royal forests so that Nehemiah could get the wood he needed for the rebuilding.

When Nehemiah first arrived in Jerusalem, he kept his mission secret. One night, as soon as he could, he went out and started to ride a donkey around the city walls. He had only gone part of the way when, because of the dark and the great heaps of rubble from the broken walls, the donkey couldn't find a safe path and came to a dead halt.

The next day, Nehemiah called together the priests and the city officials. 'Jerusalem is the city of God's people,' he said, 'but it is a terrible disgrace! It is now time to rebuild.'

Everyone agreed and the rebuilding began. Enemies began to plot to take over the city before it could be made safe against invasion, so Nehemiah gave orders that while half the men worked at

rebuilding the walls, the rest would stand guard in full armour in case of attack.

Even the workmen who were shifting building materials carried a weapon and the men laying the stones each wore a sword strapped to their waist.

When the work was finally finished, Nehemiah dedicated the city and its walls to God and a great, joyful celebration was held. All the people – men, women and children – joined in with music and singing, and the noise they made could be heard far and wide.

THE NEW TESTAMENT

26 Elizabeth and Mary

Elizabeth longed to have a baby but she knew that she was getting too old. She was married to a priest named Zechariah. One day, when he was carrying out his duties, an angel appeared to him in the most holy part of God's Temple.

Zechariah was terrified, but the angel told him not to be afraid. 'God has heard your prayers,' he said, 'and Elizabeth is going to give birth to a baby boy who will grow up to be a great man. You will call him John and he will be filled with God's Spirit like the holy men of the past. He will get people ready to meet the promised leader for whom the Jewish people have long been waiting.'

Zechariah couldn't believe his ears. 'That is impossible!' he said. 'Elizabeth and I are far too old to have a son.'

'I am Gabriel,' said the angel, 'and God has sent me with this news. But because you do not believe me, you will not be able to speak until the message I have given you comes true and the child is born.'

Zechariah came out of the Temple, but he couldn't tell anyone what had happened. The old priest went home to his wife. Not long afterwards, Elizabeth found that she was going to have a baby.

Six months later, Gabriel delivered another message, this time to a young woman named Mary, who was a cousin of Elizabeth and who lived in the town of Nazareth in Galilee.

Mary had been promised as a wife to a carpenter called Joseph, who was a descendant of David, the great king of Israel.

'Peace be with you!' said Gabriel. 'The Lord God is with you and has greatly blessed you!'

Then the angel told Mary that she was going to have a baby and that she was to name him Jesus. 'He will be great,' said Gabriel, 'and he will be a king just as David was king. His kingdom will never end.'

Mary was very frightened. 'How can such a thing happen to me,' she asked, 'when I am not yet married?'

'Your baby will be given to you by the power of God's Spirit, which is why the holy child shall be called the Son of the Most High God.'

Then Gabriel reminded Mary about her cousin. 'Everyone said that Elizabeth was too old to have a child, but now she is expecting a baby. Nothing is impossible for God.'

Mary wasn't sure what to think, but she believed Gabriel's words. 'I am God's servant,' she said. 'May everything happen as you have said.'

After Gabriel had left, Mary set out on a journey to visit her cousin Elizabeth. When the two women hugged each other, Elizabeth felt as if her baby were jumping for joy inside her.

'You have been blessed by God,' Elizabeth told Mary, 'and the child you are going to have will be greatly blessed also!'

Mary felt so happy that she began singing a song of thanks to God. 'My heart is full of joy and gladness,' she sang, 'because of the wonderful thing that God has done for me.'

Mary stayed with Elizabeth for three months before returning to Nazareth.

When Elizabeth's baby was born, the priest was going to name the boy Zechariah after his father, but Elizabeth said, 'No! His name is to be John.'

Everyone was very puzzled. 'There's no one in your family called John!' they said and asked Zechariah what he wanted the boy to be called. The old man made signs for them to give him something to write on and he wrote, 'His name is John.' At that very moment, Zechariah's voice returned and he was able to speak again.

'Let us praise the Lord God of Israel,' said Zechariah, 'because he is sending us a mighty leader who is descended from our ancestor, David. And my son will be the one to prepare the people for the coming of the king!'

27 JESUS IS BORN

When Joseph heard that the young woman he was planning to marry was going to have a baby, he was very upset and decided to break off their engagement.

But God saw that Joseph was unhappy and he sent an angel to speak to him in a dream. 'Joseph, descendant of David,' said the voice, 'do not be afraid to marry Mary, because her baby has been given to her by the Spirit of God. The child will be a boy and you will call him Jesus – and he will grow up to be the leader promised long ago to the people of Israel.'

So Joseph married Mary and they waited at their home in Nazareth for the day when this very special baby would be born.

As the day of the birth was getting close, Joseph heard the news that the Roman emperor, Caesar Augustus, had ordered that a list was to be drawn up of all the people who were living in any part of his empire.

In order to be added to the list, everyone had to travel to the town where they were born so Joseph took Mary and set out for Bethlehem, which was his home town and, many hundreds of years before, the town where King David had been born.

By the time they reached Bethlehem, Mary was about to give birth, but because of the crowds of people who were there, Joseph couldn't find anywhere for them to stay.

Mary was exhausted and Joseph was terribly worried, but wherever he tried, the story was always the same: 'No room!'

Finally they called at an inn, and although all the rooms were full, the kindly innkeeper felt sorry for the couple and told them they could stay in his stable.

That very night, watched by the cows and donkeys, Mary's baby was born; she wrapped the child up and laid him in the manger, where the straw was kept to feed the animals.

Just as God had told him to do, Joseph named the child Jesus.

Up on the hills around Bethlehem, the local shepherds were looking after their sheep when suddenly an angel appeared to them in a glorious vision of dazzling light.

The shepherds were shaking in terror when they heard a voice speaking to them out of the brightness: 'Don't be afraid!' said the angel. 'I am here with good news that will bring great joy to all people. A child has just been born in David's town – a child who has been sent to save the world! Here is the proof of what I tell you: right now, the baby is wrapped up and lying in a manger.'

In that moment, the angel was surrounded by hundreds of other angels singing a song of joy: 'Glory to God in the highest heaven, and peace on earth to those with whom he is pleased!'

When the vision faded, the shepherds talked among themselves and decided to go to Bethlehem and look for this special child that they had been told about.

Coming down from the hills, they searched everywhere in the town until they found the stable with Mary and Joseph and saw the baby Jesus asleep in the hay.

Filled with love and respect, they knelt down around the manger and looked with wonder on the little baby they had been told would one day grow to be a very great man.

As for Mary, she was careful to remember all of these things and would think about them again and again.

28 WISE MEN FROM AFAR

Around the time of Jesus' birth, wise men from the east arrived in Jerusalem. They had discovered a new star while studying the heavens and knew that it was a sign that a baby had been born who was a long-awaited king.

The king at the time was Herod. When he heard this news he was angry and frightened, and he sent for the chief priests and experts in the laws of Moses and the teachings in the holy books.

'Where is this new king to be born?' asked Herod. The advisors told him that it had been foretold that the child would be born in Bethlehem, the city where, many years before, David had been made king.

King Herod sent for the wise men and, pretending that he wanted to help them, told them to go to Bethlehem.

'Search everywhere for this important child,' he said, and then added slyly, 'and when you find him, let me know so that I can also go and worship him.'

The wise men went on with their journey. They were overjoyed when once again they saw the star, and they followed it until it led them to the place they had been seeking.

Going inside, they found Mary and the baby Jesus. At once, they knelt down before the child and presented him with gifts of gold, frankincense and myrrh.

Remembering Herod's words, the wise men were going to return to Jerusalem to tell him that they had found the child, but God told them in a dream not to go back to the king.

However, as soon as Herod realized he had been tricked, he did a terrible thing: he ordered his soldiers to kill all the newborn babies in Bethlehem and in the country around the town.

But God sent an angel to Joseph to warn him of the danger. 'Take the child and his mother,' he was told, 'and escape to Egypt. Stay there until I tell you that it is safe to leave.'

29 THE BOY JESUS

After King Herod died, God told Joseph that it was safe to leave Egypt, so he took Mary and Jesus and they went to make their home in the town of Nazareth in Galilee.

Every year, Jesus' parents went to Jerusalem to celebrate the Passover festival. When Jesus was twelve, he was allowed to go with them and all the pilgrims from Nazareth. When the festival was over, Mary, Joseph and the whole group started off for home. Without their knowing it, Jesus stayed behind in the city.

To begin with, Mary and Joseph assumed that the boy was somewhere among their family and friends. It was only after they had been travelling for a day that they began looking for him but couldn't find him anywhere. Worrying about what might have happened to their son, they finally turned around and went back to Jerusalem.

After three days of searching high and low, the anxious parents found Jesus sitting in the Temple, listening to the conversations of the Jewish teachers and asking many questions.

The teachers, who had spent many years studying the history and beliefs of their people, were all amazed by the questions the boy asked and how much he understood.

Jesus' parents were cross and hurt that Jesus had given them so much worry.

'Why did you do this to us?' asked Mary. 'When we couldn't find you, your father and I were worried to death!'

Realizing that Mary and Joseph were very upset, Jesus tried to explain. 'Why did you have to go looking for me?' he asked. 'Didn't you know that I would be in my Father's house?'

Jesus' parents didn't understand why he said this, but they were just happy to have found him safe and sound. Together once more, they set out for home.

As the years passed, the boy grew up to be a man who was strong and wise; a man who was loved by his family and friends and by God, who – as he had said when he was a child – was his heavenly Father.

30 Jesus is Baptized

When John, the son of Elizabeth and Zechariah, had grown to be a man, he put on a coat of camel hair and a leather belt and went into the desert, where he lived on wild honey and the bean pods of the locust tree.

John stayed in the desert until God told him that the time had come to start teaching people how they should live their lives.

He began speaking in public on the banks of the River Jordan and very soon, great crowds were coming from all over the area — even from the city of Jerusalem — in order to listen to him.

'It is time to stop the wicked things that you are doing,' he told the people. When they said that they would try to lead a better life, John took them into the river and baptized them as a sign that they were making a new start.

People began calling him John the Baptist and they wondered whether he might be the great leader who had long ago been promised to the Jewish people, but John told them that he was not.

'Someone is coming,' John told them, 'who is so much greater than me that I am not even good enough to untie his sandals. I only baptize you with water, but *he* will baptize you with God's Holy Spirit.'

Then, one day, Jesus came to the River Jordan and asked John to baptize him. John really didn't want to do that because he knew that this was the person he had been telling people about. 'It's not right!' he said. 'I ought to be baptized by *you*!'

'You must do as I ask,' replied Jesus kindly but firmly, 'because we must both do everything in the way that God wants it to be done.'

So John led him into the river and baptized him. As Jesus came up out of the water, something wonderful happened. It was as if the sky opened up and God's Spirit came down and settled on Jesus like a dove. Then he heard a voice from heaven that said, 'This is my own dear Son, with whom I am pleased.'

Then Jesus went away into the desert to be by himself and to think about God. After forty days and nights without food, Jesus grew very hungry. And it was then that the Evil One, whose name is Satan, found Jesus and spoke to him. 'Why go hungry?' he murmured softly. 'If you really *are* God's Son, you can order the stones at your feet to turn into bread.'

But Jesus refused to be tempted and quoted some words of the holy books: 'People cannot live on bread alone; they also need to feed on the words that God says to them.'

And then it seemed to Jesus that Satan took him up to the peak of a very high mountain and showed him all the countries in the world spread out before him.

'I can make you the ruler of everywhere and everything that you can see,' whispered Satan, 'if you will only bow down to me and honour me as being all-powerful.'

Again Jesus refused. 'I cannot do that,' he said. 'I can honour only God because only *he* is all-powerful.'

Then Satan tested Jesus one more time by putting him on the very top of the Temple in Jerusalem.

'I dare you to throw yourself off!' he said, using all his cunning. 'If you are *truly* God's Son, then surely he will send a flock of angels to catch you long before you hit the ground!'

But Jesus would not give in to Satan. 'No!' he said. 'God's word tells us that we must not test him to see if he will do what we want.'

When he heard this, Satan finally gave up tempting Jesus and left him to his thoughts.

But Jesus was not alone for long, because God sent his angels to look after his Son until it was time for him to leave the desert and to start doing the work of preaching and teaching that God had planned for him.

31 Followers of Jesus

One day, when Jesus was walking along the shore of Lake Galilee, a great many people started crowding around him, wanting him to teach them about God.

Then Jesus noticed two fishing boats pulled up on the beach and nearby, washing their nets, were four fishermen: Simon, his brother Andrew, and two more brothers named James and John.

Climbing into Simon and Andrew's boat, Jesus asked them to push it a little way out onto the lake and then sat in the boat and taught the crowds gathered on the beach.

When Jesus had finished speaking, he asked Simon and Andrew to go further out onto the lake.

'Now,' said Jesus, when they had gone a little way, 'throw out your fishing nets and see what you can catch!'

'It's no use,' said Simon. 'We worked all night long, and we didn't catch as much as a single fish!'

Then Simon looked at Jesus again and something made him change his mind.

'All right!' he said. 'If that's what you want us to do, then we will.'

The brothers lowered their nets into the water, and all at once they were swarming with hundreds of fish! In fact, the nets were so heavy that they couldn't pull them in on their own and they had to call to James and John to come and help.

Eventually both boats were loaded with so many fish that they were in serious danger of sinking!

Simon was so amazed by what had happened that he fell onto his knees in front of Jesus. 'You are such a great and powerful teacher,' he said, 'you shouldn't even be talking to someone like me, because I'm really not a very good man.'

'Do not be afraid,' said Jesus. 'I want you, Andrew, James and John to come with me and help me with my work. You have been fishermen, but from now on you are going to be fishing to catch men and women for God!'

The four men became the first of Jesus' followers. Simon was the one Jesus felt he could most rely on, and he gave him a different name – 'Peter', meaning 'a rock'. They were joined by other men until there were twelve of them in all.

There was another James and a second Simon, as well as Philip and Bartholomew, Thomas, Thaddeus and Judas.

There was also a tax collector named Matthew, who worked for the Roman authorities. One day when Matthew was sitting in his office, Jesus noticed him and went to speak to him. 'Matthew,' said Jesus, 'I want you to follow me.'

To everyone's surprise, Matthew got up, left his job and followed Jesus.

Later, Jesus was having a meal with Matthew and some of his friends when several of the religious leaders complained about the company that Jesus was keeping. 'Why does your teacher mix with these sorts of people?' they asked Jesus' other followers.

Jesus heard them and replied, 'People who are well do not need a doctor. I have not come to teach respectable people, but to tell the people no one else cares about that God loves them.'

32 JESUS THE TEACHER

One day, when Jesus and his followers were sitting on a hillside, he began teaching them about what he described as God's kingdom: a place where people could live as part of God's family, knowing that God was their Father.

In God's kingdom, Jesus said, people who are badly treated or who are sad and lonely will be happy: they will be sure of God's love and care. And people who respect and stand up for God's rules and do their best to spread peace and kindness will also share in God's happiness.

Jesus knew that some people were saying that he was trying to replace the laws that God had given to Moses. 'I have not come to do away with those laws,' said Jesus, 'but to make their teachings come true.'

Jesus then explained that he was asking people to do more than keep the laws of Moses. 'I want you to love your enemies,' he said. 'It is easy to love the friends who love *you* – even people who do not believe in God do that! I want you to love those people who *do not* love you. God makes the sun shine and the rain fall on everyone – whether they are good or bad – so if you want to please God, do what God does and treat everyone the same.'

When some of Jesus' followers asked him to teach them how to pray to God, he gave them this prayer:

'Our Father in heaven,
hallowed be your name,
your kingdom come,
your will be done,
on earth as in heaven.
Give us today our daily bread.
Forgive us our sins
as we forgive those who sin against us.
Lead us not into temptation
but deliver us from evil.'

Jesus taught his followers other things about talking to God. 'When you pray,' he said, 'do not talk loudly in public or use long words to impress anyone who is listening. Talk to God quietly and

in private, and remember that he knows everything you need, long before you ask him.'

He then explained that people worry too much about the wrong things. 'You worry about the food and drink you need to stay alive or the clothes you need to keep warm. But look at the birds: they do not sow seeds and harvest corn in order to get their food, but God still takes care of them. Look at the flowers: they do not make clothes for themselves, but God dresses them in beautiful colours as rich as those worn by any king.

'So instead of worrying about tomorrow, you should be thinking about God's kingdom and what he wants you to do with your life. God will look after everything else that you need.'

Jesus also told a story to help people understand his teaching.

'If you listen to me, and do as I tell you,' said Jesus, 'you will be like a wise man who built his house on a rock. One night, there was a great storm. The rain came lashing down, the rivers overflowed and the flood waters rose higher and higher. The wind roared and buffeted the walls of the house, but because it was built on a rock and had a strong foundation, it survived the storm.

'But if you hear what I say and then ignore it, you will be like a foolish man who built his house on the sand. When the storm came, the winds blew, the rain fell and the floods rose, but because it was built on sand that shifted this way and that, the house fell *flat*! What a catastrophe!'

33 The Hole in the Roof

Everyone wanted to hear what Jesus had to say, and wherever he went, people came from miles around to listen to him.

One day, Jesus was inside a packed house talking with some priests and religious teachers, while outside a great mass of people was crowded around the doors and windows trying to hear what was being said.

Word had got around that Jesus could help people who were unwell, and a group of friends brought a man who was paralysed, hoping that if they could reach Jesus, he might make him well again.

Because the man couldn't walk, the friends were carrying him on a bed mat. But when they reached the house, they could see that there was no way of getting even near the door, let alone *inside*. 'It's no good,' the sick man told his friends. 'Take me home again.'

The others were not going to give up that easily, so they carried the man's bed up onto the flat roof of the house and pulled off the tiles until they had made a big hole.

The people inside were really surprised when they saw a man on a bed being carefully lowered into the room right in front of where Jesus was sitting.

Touched by the friends' belief and confidence, Jesus said to the man, 'Whatever wrongs you have done, my friend, they are now forgiven.'

Some of the priests and teachers started muttering to one another, 'Who does he think he is? Only God can forgive people the wrongs they have done!'

But Jesus knew what they were thinking. 'Tell me,' he asked, 'is it easier to say, "Whatever wrongs you have done are forgiven," or to say, "Get up and walk"? But I will now prove to you that I have power from God to forgive people.'

Turning to the man, Jesus said, 'Get up, my friend, pick up your bed and go home!'

To everyone's amazement, the man got to his feet at once, picked up his bed and headed back to his home praising God for what had happened.

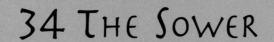

34 The Sower

Whenever Jesus taught the people, he did so by telling stories with a meaning.

One day, he told a large crowd this story:

'There was a farmer who went out into his fields to sow corn. He scattered his seeds in great handfuls, and the grains simply fell where they fell.

'Some of them landed on the footpath and were trodden on by people walking past or eaten up by the birds.

'Some fell onto rocky ground. They sprouted and began growing but soon dried up and died because there was not enough soil or moisture.

'Other seeds fell where thorn bushes were growing, and they grew up together until the thorns had choked the life out of the corn.

'But some of the seeds fell on good, rich soil. The plants made roots and grew strong and tall so that when harvest time came, the farmer had a good crop of corn.'

Jesus' followers asked him what this story meant, so he explained it for them.

'The seed,' he said, 'stands for God's word. People hear what God has to say, but – just as the farmer's seeds fell on different types of ground – people react in different ways.

'Some people are like the seeds that fell on the path. The Evil One snatches away what they hear and they simply do not believe.

'Other people are like the seeds that fell on the rocky ground.

Although they believe God's word to start with, it does not take root and as soon as things get difficult, they give up.

'Some people are like the seeds that landed among the thorn bushes. They begin to grow in their faith, but soon all the worries and cares and pleasures of the world crowd in until there is no longer any room for God.

'But then there are the people who hear God's word, follow it and never give up. They are like the seeds that fell onto the good soil in the farmer's field and grew into a crop that was tall and strong and plentiful.'

35 The Storm on the Lake

One evening, Jesus decided to cross to the other side of Lake Galilee. He and his followers got into a boat and Peter, Andrew and the others put up the sail and started making the crossing.

Once they were on their way, Jesus lay down in the back of the boat and fell fast asleep with his head on a pillow.

A little while later, when they were about halfway across the lake, the sky began to grow very dark and a great storm blew up.

Strong winds whipped up the waves, tossing the boat this way and that. Water poured over the sides of the boat and the followers began to think that they were going to sink.

Even those among Jesus' followers who had been fishermen and knew how to handle a boat became afraid; but despite everything that was going on, Jesus himself was still sound asleep.

Eventually the followers shook Jesus awake. 'Master! Master!' they shouted. 'Help us or we're all going to die!'

Jesus stood up in the boat and spoke to the storm. 'Be quiet!' he told the roaring wind, and it suddenly dropped and was silent. 'Be still!' he told the waves, and they stopped heaving the boat back and forth and became quite calm.

Then Jesus turned to his followers. 'Why were you so frightened?' he asked. 'Do you still not believe and have faith in the things that I have taught you?'

'What kind of a man is Jesus?' the followers asked themselves.

'Even the wind and the waves do what he tells them.'
The storm itself had been terrifying... but Jesus' words filled them with wonder.

36 The Little Girl

The boat with Jesus on board came in to land at a little lakeside town. A great many people were gathered on the beach waiting to meet the famous teacher.

Jesus had hardly stepped ashore when a man named Jairus started pushing his way through the crowd. When the people saw who he was they made way for him, because he was a respected person in their community.

Although he was an important person, Jairus threw himself onto the ground at Jesus' feet. 'Please help me, Teacher,' he begged in tears. 'My twelve-year-old daughter is dying. If you would only come to my house, I know that you could make her well!'

Jesus agreed to go with Jairus, but before they could reach the house, someone ran up to Jairus with a message. 'Sir, your daughter has died,' he said. 'The Teacher cannot do anything to help you now.'

Jairus was broken-hearted, but Jesus overheard the message. 'Do not be afraid,' he said calmly. 'Trust me and believe, and she will be well.'

When they arrived at the house, Jesus went inside with the child's parents and Peter, James and John.

The place was full of relatives who were crying because the little girl had died, but Jesus told them to be quiet. 'Why are you making all this noise?' he asked. 'The child is not dead – she is only sleeping!'

This only made the relatives angry: they jeered and argued, but Jesus took no notice of their complaints.

Instead, he went over to the bed where the child was lying and took her hand in his. 'Get up, my child!' he said. The girl's eyes flickered open and she sat up and smiled at her mother and father.

'Tell no one what has happened here,' Jesus told the astonished parents. Then, looking across at the little girl, he added, 'And give your daughter something to eat – she must be hungry.'

37 Loaves and Fishes

There came a time when Jesus knew that his twelve followers had learned enough from his teachings to be able to pass the message on to other people. He decided to send them out into all the towns and villages to tell others what people were now calling the Good News.

Sometime later, the followers came back and told Jesus everything that had happened and what they had done. Their preaching and their miracles had caused a great stir in all of Galilee.

Now Jesus wanted to spend some time alone with them. Together they went to a town called Bethsaida. But they could not just slip away any more. So many people had heard about Jesus that a great crowd followed him. Some wanted to ask him questions; others who were sick wanted Jesus to make them well again.

Jesus spent all day on a hillside some way outside the town, talking to the people and helping them. Then, when it got near to evening, Jesus' followers came and spoke to him.

'You should send the people away now,' they said. 'This is a lonely spot and they need to go off and find somewhere to stay before it gets dark. Besides, no one has eaten all day and they're hungry.'

'They do not have to leave,' said Jesus. 'Why not give them something to eat?'

Jesus' followers looked amazed. 'Us?' they asked. 'There must be 5,000 people here; where are we supposed to get enough money to buy food for that many people?'

Jesus waited until they had finished complaining and then asked, 'What have you got to eat between all of you?'

The followers went to check and returned with dismal news. 'All we've got is five loaves and two small fish.'

'Very well,' said Jesus. 'Bring me the food and then go and tell everyone to sit down in groups of fifty and they will be fed.'

Jesus' followers could hardly believe their ears, but they did as Jesus told them. When the crowd was sitting down, Jesus took the five loaves and the two fish and thanked God for giving them food.

Then he broke the loaves and the fish into pieces and gave them to his followers to hand around.

No one understood how it was possible, but everyone in the crowd had enough to eat. And at the end of the meal, there were still baskets of food left over.

38 The Good Samaritan

There was a teacher who was proud of himself: he knew all about the laws that God had given to Moses. One day, he came to Jesus and asked a question. He wanted to test just how wise the young preacher was – or indeed, how foolish.

'What must I do,' he enquired, 'to be part of God's kingdom?'

'What does it say in the book of the Law?' asked Jesus.

The teacher replied, 'It says, "Love the Lord your God with all your heart, with all your strength and with all your mind." It also says, "Love your neighbour as you love yourself."'

'You are right,' Jesus told him. 'Do that and you will be part of the kingdom.'

But the teacher wasn't satisfied, so he then asked, 'Who *is* my neighbour?' Jesus answered by telling the teacher this story:

'A man was travelling from Jerusalem to Jericho. Suddenly he was attacked by a gang of thieves who beat him up, stripped him, took everything he had and left him half dead by the roadside.

'Shortly afterwards, one of the Temple priests came down the road and saw the wounded man lying there. Worried that he might get mixed up in some trouble, the priest crossed over and went by on the other side.

'A little later, a man who worked in God's Temple came by and heard the wounded man moaning. He went over to look, but decided it was best not to get involved and hurried on his way.

'Finally, a man from Samaria came along. Like all Samaritans, he did not agree that the right place to worship God is at the Temple in Jerusalem. But when the Samaritan saw that someone was in need, he stopped and went to help.

'First he put oil and wine on the man's wounds and then he tore up part of his own coat in order to make bandages.

'When he had done this, he carefully lifted the man onto his donkey and took him to an inn, where he could take proper care of him.

'The next day, the Samaritan had to travel on. Before he left, he gave the innkeeper two silver coins. "Use this money," he said,

"to do whatever needs to be done to look after that man. And if you have to spend more money, I will pay you back when I next come by this way."'

Then Jesus said to the teacher, 'You asked me, "Who is my neighbour?" Tell me, in your honest opinion, which of those three men acted like a neighbour to the man who was attacked by the thieves?'

There was only one answer the teacher could give Jesus. 'The man who was kind to him,' he said.

'Yes,' replied Jesus, 'and now you know, make sure you behave in the same way.'

39 The Great Feast

One day, Jesus was invited to the home of a wealthy man. He was deeply religious, and he and his friends were anxious because they thought that Jesus did not obey the laws of Moses as strictly as he should. During the dinner, Jesus told this story:

'There was once a king who decided to give a great banquet. He sent out many invitations and made elaborate preparations. "There must be all kinds of good things to eat and drink," he told his servants.

'At last, the day of the feast came, and the king sent a servant out to remind all those who had been invited.

'The first guest that the servant called on was just leaving his house. "I've bought a piece of land," he explained, "and I have to go and look at it. So I can't possibly come. Sorry."

'The next guest also had an excuse: "I'm afraid I won't be able to come to the banquet," he said. "I've bought some oxen to plough my fields and I have to go and see them at work. Give the king my apologies."

'A third guest was having his own party. "Look!" he told the servant. "I've just got married! I'm sure the king will understand."

'And so it went on. Excuse after excuse, until the servant had to go back and tell the king that none of his invited guests would be coming.

'The king was very angry and gave his servant new orders: "Go into every street and alleyway in the town and bring back whoever you find there. It doesn't matter if they are poor or sick, whether they have anywhere to live or enough to eat. Invite them *all* to my banquet."

'The servant did as he was told, and there were still spare places at the table. So the king sent his servant off again. "Go out again – this time into the country lanes – and *make* people come in! And as for those who were invited in the beginning, not one of them will share in this feast."'

40 The Lost Son

The religious people were displeased with Jesus. 'Why does this man spend so much time with outcasts?' they grumbled. 'It's not right.'

So Jesus told this story:

'There was once a man with two sons. He promised them that everything he owned would one day be shared between them.

'The younger son, who was very impatient, didn't care much for this arrangement. "I don't want to have to wait until you're dead," he told his father. "I want my share *now*!"

'So the father divided everything then and there between his boys. Within a day or two, the younger son had sold off his share, pocketed the money and headed off in search of a good time.

'He went a long way away to another country, where he made friends with the wrong sort of people – ones who were very happy to help him spend his money! It didn't take him long to get through his share of the inheritance. All too soon he found himself without enough money even for a crust of bread.

'He took a lowly job with a farmer, looking after the pigs, but every day he went to bed hungry. In fact, he was so ravenous, he found himself thinking about finishing up the scraps in the bottom of the pig food buckets.

'One day, he came to his senses.

"The people who work for my father always have more than enough to eat," he said, "and here I am, starving! I'll go back, tell him I'm sorry and ask him to give me a job because I'm no longer good enough to be called his son." So, barefoot and dressed in rags, he set out.

'The father often watched the road on which he had waved his son goodbye. One evening, he saw what he had hardly dared dream: his son was on his way home. Rather than wait for him to arrive, he ran and grabbed the boy into his arms, and hugged and kissed him.

'The young man pulled away, ashamed. "Father," he said, "I have wronged you and wronged God. I don't deserve to be called your son."

'The father paid no attention. "Fetch clean clothes for my son," he called to the servants. "And prepare a feast. We must celebrate my son's homecoming."

'The elder brother was working in the fields, and it was only on his way back to the house that he heard the sound of laughter, music and dancing. "What's happening?" he asked one of the servants. When he heard the news, he was very angry and refused to go inside.

'His father came out and begged him to come and join the party.

' "Why should I?" asked the son. "It's not fair! I've worked for you for years and always done what I've been told, but you've never given a feast for me. And yet my brother behaves selfishly and throws your money away, and you welcome him home with open arms!"

' "Listen, my son," said his father gently. "You are always with me, and everything I have is yours; but we lost your brother and now he's been found! It's as if he was dead and is now alive again! Isn't that something we should all be happy about?" '

41 God's Kingdom

All kinds of people asked Jesus all kinds of questions and he often answered with a story.

He knew that some of those who questioned him were trying to trick him and didn't really want to hear what he had to say because they believed that they were better than anyone else. To those people, he told this story:

'There were two men who went into God's Temple to pray. One was a teacher who thought of himself as a very religious man; the other was a man who collected the tax money which people had to pay to the Romans.

'The first man stood up and started praying in a loud voice so that everyone could hear. "I thank you, God," he said, "that I am not like other people. I go without food twice a week as a sign of my obedience to you and give you a share of all my money. I thank you that I am not a money-grabbing crook like that tax collector there!"

'But the tax collector stood over to one side, looking down at the ground, and prayed quietly: "Please forgive me, God, for all the wrong things that I have done."

'I tell you,' said Jesus, 'when the two men left the Temple, only the tax collector was God's friend.

'Remember,' Jesus told those listening, 'God does not treat people in a special way just because they try to make themselves important.

Anyone who recognizes that they are just ordinary will find that they are important to God.'

A rich and important man who had been listening asked Jesus what he had to do to please God. Jesus told him that he needed to keep the laws that God gave to Moses.

'Ever since I was young,' said the man, 'I have kept all God's laws.'

'Then,' said Jesus, 'there is just one more thing that you need to do. Sell everything you have, give the money to the poor and follow me. Do that and you will *really* be a rich person!'

When the man heard this he was sad. He was so wealthy that he couldn't even begin to think of doing what Jesus asked. Instead, he turned and walked away.

'It is hard,' Jesus said, 'for a rich person to become part of God's kingdom. No one can work for two masters at the same time: if he does, he will love one and hate the other. That is why it is not possible to love both God and money.'

While Jesus was teaching, people began bringing their young children to him and asking him to bless them. Some of Jesus' followers told the people not to bother Jesus and tried to send the children away.

When Jesus heard what they were doing, he called the youngsters back. 'Let the children come to me,' he said, 'and do not ever stop them – because God's kingdom belongs to everyone who believes in it in the same way that a child believes.'

42 Jesus and Zacchaeus

Jesus and his followers were passing through Jericho on their way to Jerusalem. A huge crowd of excited people were all along the road, and right at the back was a little man named Zacchaeus, who worked as a tax collector for the Romans.

Nobody liked Zacchaeus and nobody trusted him – because he had got very rich demanding high taxes and keeping an extra large slice for himself.

Like everyone, Zacchaeus had heard about Jesus and wanted to see him, but stuck at the back of the crowd he couldn't see anything other than the backs of the people in front!

He tried pushing by people and squeezing in between them, but no one would make room for him.

Then he had an idea. He ran ahead of the crowd and climbed up into a sycamore tree that overhung the road. Now he had the perfect place from which to watch Jesus go by.

As Jesus passed under the tree, he stopped and looked up. He saw Zacchaeus, perched like a bird in the branches, and, to everyone's surprise, he called up to this little man that nobody liked.

'Come down,
Zacchaeus!'
said Jesus.
'I want to stay in
your house today.'

Zacchaeus was so
shocked that he didn't move.

'Hurry up!' called Jesus –
so the astonished Zacchaeus
scrambled down.

But the people weren't happy that
Jesus wanted to visit the house of someone
who had robbed them of their money.

Zacchaeus stood looking at Jesus and suddenly
started to feel like a new man. 'You are welcome to
come to my house,' he said, 'and I'll give away to the
poor half of everything I have.'

And then he added in a loud voice so everyone would
hear, 'And if I've cheated any of you, I'll pay you back four
times as much!'

The crowd was surprised, but Jesus told them, 'Whatever
Zacchaeus has done wrong, God has forgiven him.'

Zacchaeus kept his promises, and although he was still a little
man, people stopped looking down on him. It was almost as if
meeting Jesus had made him grow.

43 Riding to Jerusalem

Jesus decided to go to Jerusalem. When he was a little way off from the city, he sent two of his twelve followers on ahead of him to a village further down the road.

'When you get there,' he told them, 'you will find a donkey tied up, and beside her will be her young colt, which has not yet been ridden by anyone. Untie the animals and bring them here. And if anyone asks you what you are doing or why, simply say, "The Master needs them," and no one will do anything to stop you.'

So the two men went on ahead and everything happened exactly as Jesus had said.

When they returned, they put their coats over the back of the young donkey for Jesus to sit on. As he rode towards Jerusalem, a crowd began following him. Others ran on in front and covered the ground with their cloaks and with branches torn from the palm trees.

It was like a royal procession; the crowd grew bigger and bigger, and soon everyone was singing and chanting: 'Praise to King David's son! Praise to the man who comes in the name of the Lord God! Peace in heaven and glory to God!'

Eventually, Jesus and the crowd arrived at the gates of Jerusalem; as soon as they entered the city, the place was in uproar. 'Who *is* this man?' asked some of the people who didn't know Jesus. The crowd shouted back, 'It's Jesus, the teacher from Nazareth in Galilee!'

Some of the religious leaders grew worried at the number of people who were crowding the city streets and exciting everyone with their singing and shouting. 'Teacher,' they begged Jesus, 'tell your followers to be quiet.'

But Jesus shook his head. 'I tell you,' he said, 'even if the people were to be silent, all the stones in the walls and streets of Jerusalem would start shouting!'

When the procession reached the Temple, Jesus got off the donkey and went inside. What he saw upset him very much. Everywhere he looked, there were people exchanging money and buying and selling birds and animals for sacrifices. It was more like a market than a place where people go to worship God.

Jesus became so angry that he began knocking over the traders' tables. Within minutes, there were coins rolling all over the Temple floor and the air was full of pigeons flying up from the cages that had smashed open when they hit the ground.

In a loud voice, Jesus called out, 'God said, "My Temple will be called a house of prayer," but you are making it into a hideout for thieves!'

The religious leaders were very angry that Jesus had done this, but the ordinary people flocked into the Temple to listen to Jesus speak and brought friends and family who were unwell so that he could make them better.

44 THE LAST SUPPER

Each day after he arrived in Jerusalem, Jesus went to the Temple to teach; every evening, he went up onto the Mount of Olives to be alone with God.

Some of the priests and religious leaders believed that Jesus was a dangerous troublemaker, and they began plotting to get rid of him, although they didn't dare do anything when Jesus was in the Temple surrounded by crowds of people.

Then someone unexpected offered to help Jesus' enemies. One of Jesus' twelve followers, Judas Iscariot, agreed to hand Jesus over to them, and when they promised to pay him money, he began looking for an opportunity to betray Jesus.

It was time for celebrating the festival of Passover, when the Jewish people remember how God had led them out of slavery in Egypt.

Jesus and the twelve followers met to eat the Passover meal in an
upstairs room. When they were sitting at the table, Jesus said,
'I have wanted so much to eat this meal with you before I suffer.'

His followers were wondering what he meant,
when he told them something that shocked
them even more.

'One of you,' said Jesus looking round
the table, 'will betray me.'

They all began talking at once. 'Who?'
they asked. 'It's not me, is it?' The last
to ask was Judas. 'Surely, Teacher,'
he said, 'you don't mean *me*?'

Jesus simply answered,
'So you say.'

Then Jesus said a prayer
of thanks to God for the
meal they were about
to eat. Taking the
bread, he broke it
and handed it to
the others.
'Take and
eat it,' he
said.
'This is
my body.'

When they had shared the bread, Jesus took a cup of wine and, after another prayer of thanks, handed it to his followers to be passed around. 'Drink it, all of you,' he said. 'This is my blood, which guarantees God's promise to forgive people for all the wrongs they have done.'

When the meal was finished, all of them except Judas went with Jesus to the Mount of Olives.

On the way, Jesus began telling his friends things that, at the time, they didn't understand. 'This very night,' he said, 'all of you will run away and leave me.'

Peter was quick to reply. 'I will *never* leave you!' he said firmly. 'Even if all the others do, I never shall!'

Jesus looked Peter in the eyes. 'I tell you, Peter,' he said, 'before the cock crows, you will say three times that you do not even know me.'

Peter was hurt. 'I will never say that,' he said angrily, 'even if I have to die with you!'

When they reached a garden on the Mount of Olives called Gethsemane, Jesus told his followers to sit and wait for him. Taking Peter, James and John, he walked further on.

'I am very sad,' Jesus told his three friends, 'and I feel as if I am being crushed by my unhappiness. Please stay close by and keep watch while I pray to my Father.'

Jesus went on a little way alone and knelt down. 'Father,' he prayed, 'I feel as if I were being offered a drink from a cup that is full of pain and suffering.'

Then, in tears, Jesus asked, 'If it is possible, Father, please do not let me be handed this cup. But if it is what you want to happen, then I will do as you ask.'

Jesus talked with God for an hour, and when he came back, he found Peter, James and John sound asleep with tiredness and worry.

'Wake up!' he called. 'Could you not keep awake for just one hour?'

His friends were upset. 'You mean well in your hearts,' said Jesus, 'but the human body is weak. Ask God to keep you from giving way to temptation. Come now, it is time to go.'

And as he spoke, they saw a lot of people with burning torches making their way up the path towards the garden.

45 The Crucifixion

Judas arrived in the garden of Gethsemane with some of the religious leaders and a crowd of men carrying swords and sticks. He went straight up to Jesus and kissed him.

This was the signal that the crowd had been waiting for and they immediately grabbed Jesus.

'Judas,' said Jesus, 'do you betray me with a kiss?'

Then, turning to the crowd, he said, 'Did you really have to come with weapons to catch me in the night as if I were an outlaw? I was with you every day in the Temple and you never tried to arrest me!'

Jesus was led off towards the city and, just as he had said would happen, his friends ran away. Only Peter followed, at the very back of the crowd, to see what would happen.

When they reached the house of the high priest, Peter sat down by a fire in the courtyard. While he was sitting there, first one person and then another asked if he was a friend of Jesus, but each time he said, 'No!'

The third time he was asked, Peter said, 'Listen, I've no idea what you're talking about!' But he had hardly finished speaking when a cock crowed and he remembered that Jesus had said that he would deny knowing him three times.

In the morning, the priests and religious teachers questioned Jesus and asked him if he was the great king who had long been promised to the Jewish people.

'If I tell you,' replied Jesus, 'you will not believe me.'

'Are you the Son of God?' they demanded. Jesus answered, 'You say that I am.'

So they took Jesus to Pontius Pilate, the Roman governor, and demanded that Jesus be put to death because his claims to be the promised king would cause trouble and riots throughout the country.

Pilate asked Jesus, 'Are you the king of the Jews?' And again Jesus replied, 'So you say.'

Although Pilate didn't want to upset the religious leaders, he believed that Jesus was innocent.

Hoping to set Jesus free, Pilate took him out to the people and asked them what he should do. But the crowd was full of Jesus' enemies and they yelled at the top of their voices, *'Crucify him! Crucify him!'*

Finally, Pilate gave in and handed Jesus over to the Roman guards. They whipped him and then made fun of him by dressing him up in a purple robe and making him a crown of branches of thorn. Bowing down to him, they shouted, 'Long live the king of the Jews!'

Then the soldiers led Jesus away to a place outside the walls of Jerusalem where criminals were executed.

Jesus was nailed to a cross of wood by his hands and feet, and left to hang there until he died. Despite the terrible pain, Jesus prayed for his executioners. 'Forgive them, Father!' he called out. 'They don't know what they are doing.'

A notice was fixed to the cross saying, 'This is the king of the Jews.' Two thieves were crucified with Jesus, one on either side of him, and one of them called out, 'If you're really the Son of God, save yourself and us!'

But the other thief said, 'We deserve our punishment, but Jesus has done nothing wrong.' Then he said to Jesus, 'Remember me when you are king.'

Jesus replied, 'I promise that today you will be with me in my Father's kingdom.'

The Roman soldiers on duty at the foot of the cross gambled with dice for Jesus' clothes and many of his enemies came by to laugh at his suffering.

Storm clouds filled the sky and for three hours the sun never shone.

Among the crowd, Jesus saw his mother Mary holding on to the arm of John, who was one of his twelve followers. Looking at them and seeing how sad they were, Jesus said, 'Mother, John is now your son. John, she is now your mother.'

And from that day, John took Mary to live in his house.

Jesus asked for a drink, so a soldier filled a sponge with wine, put it on a stick and lifted it up to his lips.

Then Jesus spoke for the last time. 'It is finished,' he said. Then he bowed his head and died.

46 THE EMPTY TOMB

As soon as Jesus had been sentenced to die, Judas realized what a terrible thing he had done and went to the religious leaders who had given him money to hand Jesus over to them.

'I have sent an innocent man to his death!' he said and he tried to give back the thirty pieces of silver that he had been paid.

'That's your business, not ours!' the leaders replied, refusing the money.

Judas threw the coins onto the Temple floor and, deeply ashamed of what he had done, he went and hanged himself.

There was a man named Joseph who was one of the religious teachers who had cross-examined Jesus but had disagreed with what had been done to him. After Jesus had died on the cross, Joseph went to Pontius Pilate and asked if he could take care of Jesus' body.

Pilate gave his permission, and Joseph, helped by some of Jesus' friends, including a group of women followers, took down the body from the cross and wrapped it in a linen sheet. Then they carried Jesus' body to a garden where there was a tomb carved out of the rocks – a tomb that Joseph had bought for his own burial when his time came to die.

Joseph laid the body of Jesus in the tomb, which was closed up with a large stone rolled across the entrance.

All this happened on a Friday; the next day was the Jewish holy day when nobody worked.

Very early on the Sunday morning, just as the day was dawning, the women set off for the tomb with special spices and perfumes that they had prepared to put on Jesus' body.

As they went, the women were wondering how they could get help to roll the stone away from the entrance to the tomb; but when they reached the garden, they were shocked and astonished to find that it had already been moved. The tomb was open, and when they went in, they found that it was empty.

While they were puzzling over this, two men in shining clothes appeared nearby. The women were terribly afraid and bowed down to them, wondering what it could mean.

Then the men, who were angels, spoke and asked, 'Why are you looking among the dead people for someone who is alive? Jesus is not here. He has risen!'

The women went back at once to tell the news to Jesus' eleven followers, but when the men heard the story they thought the women were talking nonsense and refused to believe them.

Peter, however, decided to go and see for himself. He ran to the garden, and when he looked inside the tomb, he saw the linen cloth that had been wrapped around Jesus' body, but no sign of Jesus.

Realizing that something very wonderful had happened, Peter went home, hardly daring to believe that what he had seen was true.

47 THE ROAD TO EMMAUS

On the day the women found the tomb empty, two of Jesus'
followers were going from Jerusalem to a village named Emmaus.

They were talking over everything that had happened when
a stranger joined them.

'What are you talking about?' the stranger asked.

'Well,' said one of the two, named Cleopas, 'you must be the
only visitor to Jerusalem who doesn't know the things that have
been happening!'

'What things?' asked the man.

'About Jesus of Nazareth,' said Cleopas. 'He was a good man,
loved by God and the people, and we hoped that he was the
promised king; but he was treated like a criminal, sentenced
to death and crucified.'

'What's more,' added Cleopas's companion, 'this morning some of the women in our group went to where Jesus was buried and couldn't find his body. Others say they have seen his tomb and that it's empty. So now we don't know what to believe.'

The stranger looked at the two. 'You should believe that all these things happened,' he said, 'because they were meant to happen and were written about years ago by Moses and other wise men.'

As they walked, the stranger taught Cleopas and his companion many things. It was almost dark when they reached Emmaus and they persuaded the man to join them for a meal.

When they were sitting at the table, the stranger took a loaf of bread, said a blessing and broke it into pieces. That was when they realized who he was. It was Jesus!

It was as if they had been blind and could suddenly see, but just as they recognized him, he disappeared from sight.

The two went straight back to Jerusalem to tell the others what had happened. While they were telling their story, Jesus was suddenly standing in the room with them.

'Peace be with you,' he said.

Everyone was terrified and thought that they were seeing a ghost. 'Do not be afraid!' said Jesus. 'See the wounds left by the nails. Touch me, feel me, and you will see that I am real. Ghosts are not made of flesh and bone!'

Then Jesus said, 'I have work for you all. When I am with God my Father, I will send you heavenly strength to do the things I am going to ask of you. I want you to tell everyone that I died and came back from the dead so that God would forgive all the wrong and wicked things that people have done. This is a message for the whole world and you will tell it to them.'

Then Jesus led them out of Jerusalem. When they were a little way from the city, he raised up his hands and blessed them; as he was doing so, he left them and they saw him no longer.

Then Jesus' followers returned to Jerusalem and went to the Temple to praise God and give thanks for everything that Jesus had taught them.

48 God's Holy Spirit

After Jesus had returned to his heavenly Father, the eleven
faithful followers went back to Jerusalem. There they found
a place to stay and often met with other friends of Jesus to pray.
Jesus' own mother, Mary, was one of the group of more than
a hundred.

There was one important thing they had to agree on together:
how to replace Judas. They asked God to guide them in making the
choice, and in this way picked a man named Matthias. He had been
with the group since the earliest days and had heard all of Jesus'
teachings.

Now once again there were twelve chosen followers. They
knew that they were the ones who were going to be responsible
for carrying on the work that Jesus had begun and telling the story
of his life, death and resurrection to those who had not yet heard
the Good News. But they were still waiting for the right time and
for the heavenly strength that Jesus had promised.

Fifty days after the festival of Passover came the harvest festival
called Pentecost. Jerusalem was crowded with pilgrims from many
different countries who had come to worship at the Temple. Jesus'
followers were meeting in a house when, suddenly, everybody heard
a great noise coming from the sky that sounded as if a mighty wind
was blowing. The sound roared and blasted into the room and
seemed to be filling the whole house.

Then everyone there saw what looked like flames of fire, spreading out and touching each of them. In that moment, the people in the room were taken over by the Holy Spirit of God and they began talking in different languages.

There was so much noise that a great crowd gathered to see what was going on. What they heard astonished them because even though they came from various parts of the world, each and every one of them heard the story of Jesus as if it were being told in their own language.

The people in the crowd were staggered and rather frightened. 'What does it mean?' they asked. 'These are ordinary folk from

Galilee. They don't speak our language and we don't speak theirs, and yet we can all understand everything they are saying!'

Some people poked fun, saying, 'They've just had too much to drink!' But then Peter stood up with the other eleven followers and, in a loud voice, spoke to the crowd.

'Let me tell you what this all means,' said Peter. 'These people are not drunk – it's only nine o'clock in the morning! No! We have been filled with the Spirit of God, as was promised long ago by the writers of the holy books. This has happened so that we can tell all of you what God has done for us and for all the world.'

Then Peter went on to tell them about Jesus. 'Listen!' said Peter. 'Jesus of Nazareth was a man of God. You know this for yourselves because you heard him speak and you saw the miracles that he did. He was handed over to wicked men who crucified him, but you all killed him by letting them do it.

'So Jesus died and was buried, but God brought him back to life and we have all seen him! Now Jesus has joined his Father and we have been given God's Holy Spirit. What you see and hear today is that gift, which has now been passed on to us.

'These are the things that you must understand: God promised that he would make a king of one of David's descendants and that king was Jesus – the man you crucified.'

When the people heard this, they were very upset. 'What shall we do?' they asked.

'Each one of you,' said Peter, 'must stop doing the wrong things that you do and be baptized in the name of Jesus so that you can be forgiven for past wrongs and be given God's Holy Spirit. This is God's promise and it has been given to you and your children and to everyone, everywhere.'

That day, 3,000 people were baptized and joined Jesus' followers and friends.

Peter and the others taught in the Temple and, by the power given to them by Jesus, healed people who were sick. And every day, as the weeks went by, the number of people who believed in Jesus grew and grew.

49 STEPHEN'S FAITH

So many people started believing in what they heard about Jesus that very soon Peter and the other followers realized that they needed help with their work.

They chose and blessed seven helpers, including a man named Stephen, who everyone could see had God's Holy Spirit in his life.

Stephen began teaching, and before long made powerful enemies who argued with him, but because he was so wise, they could never get the better of him.

Because Stephen's enemies were determined to stop him from teaching, they bribed people to spread lies about him.

Eventually, Stephen was dragged before the senior religious leaders to answer these accusations.

The paid witnesses told their lies. 'This man is always saying things against Moses and God,' said one. Another said, 'I heard Stephen say that Jesus of Nazareth will tear down God's Temple!'

Then the high priest asked Stephen, 'Is this true?'

Stephen spoke for a long time, reminding his listeners of the history of their religion. He talked about the faithfulness of Abraham, Jacob and Joseph, the laws that God gave to Moses and the promises made to Joshua, David and Solomon.

'You are so stubborn!' said Stephen as he came to the end of what he had to say. 'In the past, people killed God's messengers who announced the coming of the great king who was God's servant.

Now you have betrayed and murdered the king himself.'

The religious leaders grew very angry, but Stephen knew that he was right, and looking up, he saw a wonderful vision. 'I see God's glory,' he said, 'and his Son, Jesus, standing beside him!'

This was too much for his enemies and they seized him and dragged him out of the city.

Then, giving their cloaks to a man named Saul to hold, they started pelting Stephen with stones.

Just before he died, Stephen cried out to God, 'Father, take my spirit and forgive them for what they have done!'

Saul watched all this and approved of what had been done to Stephen.

50 TELLING THE NEWS

Saul hated the followers of Jesus! He did everything in his power to stop them spreading the news that Jesus was God's Son. Saul had watched Stephen being stoned to death and was ready to see the same thing done to others.

Because this new religion was spreading beyond Jerusalem, Saul asked the high priest to give him power to go to the city of Damascus and arrest people who believed in the resurrection of Jesus.

Saul was travelling along the road to Damascus when suddenly there was a blinding flash of light and he fell to the ground.

As he lay on the ground, Saul heard a voice saying, 'Saul, Saul, why do you hound me and my followers?'

'Who are you?' asked Saul.

'I am Jesus!' said the voice. 'Now go into the city, where you will be told what you must do.'

When Saul tried to get up, he realized that he couldn't see, so his fellow travellers led him into Damascus, where he spent three days unable to see and going without food or drink.

While Saul was praying to God day and night, Jesus appeared in a dream to a man named Ananias and told him to go to find Saul and, with God's power, give him back his sight.

Ananias could hardly believe his ears because he had heard all about what Saul had done to Jesus' followers.

'I want you to go,' said Jesus, 'because I have chosen Saul to work for me and to make my name known – not just to the people of Israel but also to people who are not Jewish.'

So Ananias went and found Saul, placed his hands on him and told him what Jesus had said. At once, Saul could see again and he stood up and asked to be baptized as a follower of Jesus.

When Saul talked about believing in Jesus, he himself became hated. His new enemies hatched a plot to kill him. So one night, Saul's friends lowered him in a basket down the city wall in order that he could escape.

Jesus' story continued to spread and some of the men he had chosen when he began his work wrote down their memories of the things he had said and done.

Others travelled around teaching people about Jesus' life and how he was the Son of God; Saul – who had changed his name to Paul –

in particular began a series of long journeys to spread the Good News and had many adventures and met with all kinds of dangers on the way.

Jesus' followers were sometimes beaten, arrested and imprisoned by their enemies and some of them were even killed because of what they believed.

But God never let their work go to waste and, wherever they went, more and more people were baptized as believers and gathered together in groups that were the first churches.

To help the churches learn more about Jesus and the way in which he wanted them to live their lives, the first followers wrote them letters that were full of advice, wisdom and encouragement.

Again and again, they reminded their readers that Jesus' life and death were a sign of God's great love.

One of them, named John, wrote this: 'Let us love one another because love comes from God, and everyone who shows love knows God and is his child. God *is* love and he showed his love by sending Jesus into the world to live and die for us so that, if we believe in him, God will forgive us for all the wrong things that we do and fill our lives with his perfect love.'

These writings by Jesus' friends and followers are still being read almost 2,000 years after they were written; and the story of how God's Son was born in a stable in Bethlehem and died a criminal's death in Jerusalem but then came back from the dead is now known to many millions of people the whole world over.